THE WAY OF SAINT JAMES
(Chemin de Saint-Jacques de Compostelle)

LE PUY TO THE PYRENEES
A Walker's Guide

About the Author

A chance viewing of a television programme in the early 1970s led to Alison's interest in the Pilgrim Road to Santiago, at that time barely known in Britain. A walker most of her life she had the opportunity to walk the 1000-mile camino from Le Puy-en-Velay to Santiago all in one go in 1990, a time which coincided, fortuitously, with Cicerone looking for an author to write an original guide in English to the Spanish section of the route. Since then Alison has walked and explored many of the pilgrim roads through Europe (France, Germany, Switzerland, Portugal) as well as those she has written about. She is the author of a forthcoming two-volume Cicerone guide to the Via Francigena, the historic pilgrim route from Canterbury to Rome.

Alison is a former teacher of French, German and Spanish to adults and her other interests include playing the French horn.

Other Cicerone guides by the author
The Way of St James – Pyrenees–Santiago–Finisterre
The Via Francigena: Part 1 – Canterbury to the Great St Bernard Pass

THE WAY OF SAINT JAMES
(Chemin de Saint-Jacques de Compostelle)

LE PUY TO THE PYRENEES
A Walker's Guide

by
Alison Raju

2 POLICE SQUARE, MILNTHORPE, CUMBRIA LA7 7PY
www.cicerone.co.uk

© Alison Raju 2003, 2010
Second edition 2010. Reprinted 2012 (with updates)

ISBN: 978 1 85284 608 4
First edition 2003
ISBN 10: 1 85284 371 3
ISBN 13: 978 1 85284 371 7

An earlier guide to the whole of this route by the same author was published as
The Way of St James: Le Puy to Santiago in 1999, ISBN: 1 85284 271 7.

A catalogue record for this book is available from the British Library.
Printed by KHL Printing, Singapore

All photographs are by the author, unless otherwise stated.
Maps drawn by Harvey Map Services.

Dedication
For all those who begin the journey as a long-distance walk and end it as a pilgrimage

Acknowledgements
I would like to thank Marigold Fox for her assistance in compiling Appendix D
and Graham Scholes for proofreading the entire text.

Advice to Readers
While every effort is made by our authors to ensure the accuracy of
guidebooks as they go to print, changes can occur during the lifetime of
an edition. If we know of any, there will be an Updates tab on this book's
page on the Cicerone website (www.cicerone.co.uk), so please check before
planning your trip. We also advise that you check information about such
things as transport, accommodation and shops locally. Even rights of way
can be altered over time. We are always grateful for information about
any discrepancies between a guidebook and the facts on the ground, sent
by email to info@cicerone.co.uk or by post to Cicerone, 2 Police Square,
Milnthorpe LA7 7PY, United Kingdom.

Front cover: Conques cathedral, detail of tympanum (Photo: Marigold Fox)

CONTENTS

Pilgrim Roads to Santiago through France and Spain

Paris

Vézelay

Tours

Via Turonensis

Via Lemovicensis

Limoges

Le Puy-en-Velay

Atlantic Ocean

Bordeaux

Via Podensis

Arles

Finisterre

Santiago

Saint-Jean-Pied-de-Port

Via Tolosana

Toulouse

León

Roncesvalles

Camino Francés

Pamplona

Astorga

Puente la Reina

Jaca

Burgos

Via de la Plata

Seville

Mediterranean Sea

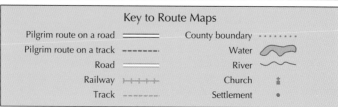

Key to Route Maps

Pilgrim route on a road	═══	County boundary	· · · · ·
Pilgrim route on a track	- - - -	Water	
Road	────	River	
Railway	┼┼┼┼	Church	⛪
Track	- - - -	Settlement	●

INTRODUCTION

PILGRIM ROADS TO SANTIAGO THROUGH FRANCE AND SPAIN

The Way of St James as described in this book and its sequel covering the section through Spain is a long-distance footpath with a difference.

People have been walking it – as a pilgrimage route – for over a thousand years, and in 1987 the section from the Spanish monastery at Roncesvalles in the foothills of the Pyrenees to Santiago de Compostela became the first European Cultural Itinerary. The 1500km route, from Le Puy-en-Velay in the Haute Loire to the City of the Apostle in the western reaches of Galicia, has changed little in all that time. For although parts of it have now become modern tarred roads, and many of its 'hospitals' and other accommodation set up by religious orders along the way to minister to the needs of pilgrims have long since disappeared, the route through France – and the *camino* as it is known in Spain – still pass through most of the same villages, climb the same hills, cross the same rivers and visit the same chapels, churches, cathedrals and other monuments as did the path taken by our predecessors in centuries gone by.

The Way of St James is also a long-distance footpath with a difference in that many of those who walk the route through France and the vast majority of those who start on the Spanish side of the Pyrenees are not experienced walkers at all. Many have never done any serious walking in their lives and many will never do any again; for here, as in the past, walking is a means of transport, a means to an end, rather than an activity for its own sake.

Most long-distance footpaths in Britain, for example, avoid not only large towns but also even quite small villages; the Way of St James, on the other hand, because of its historic origins and the need for shelter, deliberately seeks them out. Several thousand people walk the Way every year, whether from points on the *camino* in Spain, from the Pyrenees, from different parts of France, or from even further afield. It is not uncommon, even nowadays, to meet Swiss, German, Belgian or Dutch pilgrims, for example, who have set out from home to make the entire journey on foot in one go.

The modern pilgrim

However, one of the differences between the modern pilgrim and his historical counterpart, whether he walks, goes by bicycle or on horseback, is that very few return home by the same means of transport. The modern pilgrim route has thus become a 'one-way street' and it is unusual, today, to encounter anyone with either enough time or the inclination to return

View back over Conques (Section 1)

to their point of departure by the same means as they used on their outward journey.

People make the journey from Le Puy-en-Velay to the Pyrenees and then on to Santiago for a variety of reasons. For some it is just another long-distance walk. For others the motives may be historical, cultural or religious, while for many it may also be a significant action or event in their lives: to mark their retirement, perhaps, to fill the gap between studying and taking a first job or to take time out to decide which way to go next after a turning point of some sort. In the 21st century, pilgrims are people of all ages and from all walks of life. The majority of those on the Le Puy route are from France, Switzerland, Belgium, Holland and Germany, but pilgrims come from all over the world, including a relatively small number from Britain.

Some travel alone, some in twos and threes, some in large groups (particularly those on foot). Many complete the entire journey in one stretch, which helps to maintain the feel of a genuine pilgrimage, rather than a series of walking holidays. Other walkers, with more limited time, cover a section at a time over several years. But almost everyone who has walked the Way of St James, and especially those who did the whole route in one go, would probably agree that it has changed their lives in some way, even though that may not have been their original intention.

HISTORY

Pilgrims have been travelling to Santiago de Compostela on foot or on horseback (and more recently by bicycle) for over a thousand years. Godescalc, Bishop of Le Puy, who went there in AD951, was one of the first. At the height of its popularity in the 11th and 12th centuries over half a million people are said to have made the pilgrimage from different parts of Europe each year, the majority of them from France.

Pilgrimages had been popular with Christians ever since Constantine the Great had the Church of the Holy Sepulchre built over the site of Christ's burial in Jerusalem in AD326, and the discovery, shortly afterwards, of the Holy Cross itself. Those journeying to this shrine were known as *palmeros* (palmers). *Romeros* went to Rome, the burial place of Saint Peter and the other great centre of Christian pilgrimage in the Middle Ages, along with Santiago de Compostela after the finding of the remains of Saint James the Great (son of Zebedee, brother of John and Christ's cousin).

The high point of this third pilgrimage occurred between the years 1000 and 1500. But although numbers dwindled after that due to the Reformation and other, political, factors, the stream of pilgrims trudging westwards from different parts of Europe to the far reaches of Galicia in north-west Spain never completely dried up, and since the late 20th century has been experience something of a resurgence.

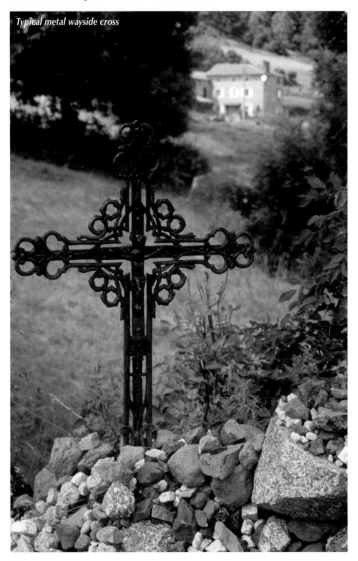

Typical metal wayside cross

The numbers of pilgrims on the Spanish section of the route has increased astronomically in the last decade (from some 4000–5000 per year in 1990 to over 180,000 in the 2004 Holy Year), and the number of pilgrims along the Le Puy route has also increased steadily; in 2008 over 10,000 pilgrims, both walkers and cyclists, were recorded as having attended the mass with pilgrim blessing held each morning in the cathedral in Le Puy, although not all of them would have continued all the way to Santiago in one go.

Legend

After the death of Christ, the disciples dispersed to different parts of the then known world, to spread the Gospel as they had been bidden. Little is known about the life of St James, but he went to Spain, where he spent a couple of years evangelising, apparently without a great deal of success. He returned to Jerusalem but was beheaded by Herod shortly afterwards, in AD44.

Immediately following his martyrdom, his followers are said to have taken his body to Jaffa, on the coast, where a ship was miraculously waiting for them and they set off back to Spain. They landed in Iria Flavia on the coast of Galicia, present-day Padrón, some 20km from what is now Santiago de Compostela, after a journey (in a *stone* boat!) which is purported to have taken only a week, thereby providing proof of angelic assistance. The body was buried in a tomb on a hillside, along with two of his disciples later on, and forgotten for the next 750 years.

Early in the 9th century Pelagius, a hermit living in that part of Spain, had a vision (which he subsequently reported to Theodomir, bishop of Ira Flavia) in which he saw a very large bright star, surrounded by a ring of smaller ones, shining over a deserted spot in the hills. The matter was investigated and a tomb containing three bodies was found there, immediately identified as those of St James and two of his followers.

When Alfonso II, King of the Asturias (791–824), went there he declared St James the patron saint of Spain. He built a church and a small monastery over the tomb in the saint's honour, around which a town grew up. It was known as *campus de la stella* or *campus stellae*, later shortened to *compostela* – one explanation of the origin of the name. Another is that it derives from the Latin *componere* (to bury), as a Roman cemetery or early Christian necropolis is known to have existed under the site of the present-day cathedral in Santiago – where the remains of St James are still believed to be housed today.

Establishing the pilgrimage

News of the discovery soon spread. It was encouraged to do so, both by Archbishop Gelmírez and the cathedral authorities (anxious to promote the town as a pilgrimage centre, thus attracting money to the area), and by the monks of Cluny (who saw in it the opportunity to assist the Spanish church in their long struggle against the Moors). Both factions were also helped by the fact that the Turks had seized the Holy Sepulchre in 1078, thus putting a stop to pilgrimages to Jerusalem.

However, Santiago was attractive as a potential pilgrim 'venue' in other respects too, as it fulfilled the various criteria necessary to make a pilgrimage there worthy of merit. It was far away (from most parts of France, for example) and difficult to reach, thus requiring a good deal of hardship and endurance to get there (and back again). It was sufficiently dangerous (wolves, bandits, fever, rivers that were difficult to cross, unscrupulous ferrymen) as well as being in Spain, then locked tight in a struggle with the Moors, and for this reason many pilgrims travelled in quite large groups. (A considerable corpus of pilgrim songs from previous centuries still exists, sung by the pilgrims as they walked.)

Modern medallion of St James as a pilgrim, Le Puy

The road itself, both through France and in Spain, was also well supplied with shrines, relics and other sights worth seeing. As pilgrim numbers increased roads, bridges and hospices were built. The pilgrimage churches were characterised by their ambulatories round the inside of the building to facilitate viewing of the relics exposed behind the high altar and were endowed with a growing number of relics, ensuring that pilgrims would pass that way to see them. Many churches in Spain are dedicated to St James, though there are very few today along the Le Puy route through France. Many others contain his statue, whether as apostle (*Saint-Jacques apôtre*) or pilgrim (*Saint-Jacques pèlerin*). In Spain there is a third, important representation: St James the Moor-slayer, or *Santiago matamoros,* though there are only very few examples of this category in France. He is featured in paintings and stained glass too, with a halo as St James the Apostle, and without when he is portrayed as a pilgrim.

There are also a considerable number of very tiny chapels along the way that are dedicated to St Roch, the pilgrim saint from Montpellier. After a pilgrimage to Rome he devoted his life to caring for plague victims, but withdrew to live in a forest when he contracted a disease which left him with an unsightly sore on his left thigh. (For this reason St Roch is depicted in art with the front flap of his coat turned back, to

Pilgrim information board in the Lozère

warn people to keep away from him, and is accompanied by the faithful dog – who brought the saint his daily rations – often with a loaf of bread in his mouth.)

Legend has confused him with *Saint-Jacques pèlerin* at times and he appears not infrequently in a 'pilgrim version' as well, with added hat, staff and scallop shells on his clothing, and there are many representations of him along the Le Puy route. Many churches and chapels of St James changed their dedication in the 16th and 17th centuries in recognition of Saint Roch's role in curing plague victims. This explains the apparent scarcity of churches and chapels of St James along the route from Le Puy to the Pyrenees today, in contrast to the pilgrim road through Spain.

Why make a pilgrimage?

People went on pilgrimages for a variety of reasons: as a profession of faith, for instance; as a form of punishment (a system of fixed penalties for certain sins was in operation during the Middle Ages); as a means of atonement; as a way of acquiring merit (and thus, for example, reducing or, in certain cases, cutting in half, the amount of time spent in Purgatory); or as an opportunity to venerate the relics of the many saints available along the principal routes to Santiago. (Indulgences were available to those who visited shrines.) No doubt, too, there were some who were just glad of the opportunity to escape their surroundings.

Later there were professional pilgrims who would (for a fee) undertake to do the pilgrimage on behalf of

13

Brick dovecote in the Quercy

affairs in order. He (or she) obtained his credentials (pilgrim passport) from his bishop or church, which he could then present in order to obtain food and lodging in the many pilgrim 'hospitals' and other establishments along the way. This was both a precaution against the growing number of *coquillards* or pseudo-pilgrims and a means of providing proof of his journey. He had his papers stamped at different stages along the way so that once he arrived in Santiago he could obtain his *Compostela* or certificate of pilgrimage from the Cathedral authorities there. This in turn entitled him to stay in the pilgrim shelters on his return journey as well as furnishing evidence, if needed, that he had actually made the pilgrimage successfully.

The pilgrim had his staff and scrip (knapsack) blessed in church before setting out and travelled light, carrying little else but a gourd for water. The scallop shell – the *coquille Saint-Jacques* – which has for many people become an essential ingredient of 'pilgrim uniform' nowadays was, in former times, something that was carried **back** from Santiago by the returning pilgrim; scallops were only found on the Galician coast and served as additional proof that the pilgrim had reached his or her destination.

The scallop shell was also the symbol embedded above doorways and elsewhere on the many and varied buildings that accommodated pilgrims along the different roads to

someone else who could afford the money but not the time to do it him- or herself. Those with the means to do so went on horseback, and some wealthy people made the pilgrimage along with a considerable retinue. The majority of pilgrims went on foot, however, and even among the rich there were some who preferred to walk rather than ride, because of the greater 'merit' they would attain.

The mediaeval experience

The pilgrim in former times was not at all sure that he would reach his destination, let alone return home in one piece, so before setting out he took leave of his family and employer, made his will and generally put his

Santiago. Pilgrims with money could stay in inns and other publicly available lodgings, but the vast majority probably stayed in the various hospices and other facilities provided for them.

Some of these were in towns (either in the centre, or outside the walls to cater both for latecomers and possibly contagious pilgrims). Others were in the countryside, often by bridges or at the crossings of important pilgrim route feeder roads: examples are the former hospital by the Pont d'Artigues near Saint-Antoine, run by the Order of the Knights of Santiago, the Chapelle d'Abrin, shortly before La Romieu, and the surviving part of the Commandery of St John of Jerusalem at the junction of the route from Le Puy and the road from Moissac to Aire-sur-l'Adour via Agen.

Much of the pilgrim accommodation was provided by religious orders, such as the Benedictines and the Antonins, and by churches and civic authorities as well as by benevolent individuals. The facilities offered varied considerably from one establishment to another, and surviving records from many of them indicate exactly what was provided for the pilgrim.

There are different explanations as to the origin of the *coquille Saint-Jacques*, but one is that when the followers of St James arrived in the port of Iria Flavia with the apostle's body they saw a man riding along the beach (a bridegroom in some versions). His horse took fright and plunged into the sea. When the pair re-emerged both horse and rider were covered from head to foot in scallop shells (even today the beaches in this part of Galicia are strewn with them).

It was customary to set out in the springtime in order to reach Santiago for the feast of St James on 25 July and return home for the winter. This was especially true in Holy Years, when 25 July falls on a Sunday (the

13th century tympanum frieze

next ones are in 2010, 2021, 2027 and 2032 – a pattern of 6–11–6–5 years), the only time the *Puerta Santa* or Holy Door of the Cathedral of Santiago is open. The door is sealed up at the end of each Holy Year and then symbolically broken down again by the Archbishop in a special ceremony in the evening of 31 December preceding the new Holy Year. The Holy Year has also always been a year in which which special concessions and indulgences were, and still are, available to pilgrims.

The first guidebook

On returning home many joined confraternities of former pilgrims in their own countries, the forerunners of the modern-day associations of 'Friends of St James' that now exist in several countries to support, promote and encourage the different routes to Santiago.

Many pilgrims then wrote accounts of their experiences, but as early as the 12th century the first real 'travel guide' was produced, probably between 1140 and 1150. Its author was for a long time believed to be one Aimery Picaud, a cleric from Parthenay-le-Vieux in the Poitou region of France, and it formed part of a Latin manuscript known as the *Codex Calixtinus*. Rather than a description of the journey of one particular individual, it was the first pilgrimage book intended to be used as a guide by prospective (especially French) pilgrims.

This book describes the four most important roads through France (see below) and divides the route from the Pyrenees to Santiago into 13 somewhat unequal stages. It lists, with comments, the places through which the route passes in Spain, indicates some of the hazards pilgrims may encounter and contains advice on the rivers along the way, indicating which are safe to drink from and which should be avoided.

The author also describes in some detail the inhabitants of the different regions through which the prospective pilgrim will pass, their language (including one of the earliest lists of Basque words), customs and characteristics, none of which compare at all favourably, in his opinion, with those of the people of his native Poitou. He includes a list of shrines to be visited along the different roads through France, a description of the city of Santiago and its churches and a detailed account of the Cathedral's history, architecture and canons.

It is now thought that this guide was not written by one person but was a compilation, designed (under the influence of the energetic Archbishop Diego Gelmírez) to promote Santiago de Compostela as a pilgrimage centre. Regardless of its authorship, this guide was certainly instrumental in popularising the itineraries of the four main pilgrim roads through France and the *Camino Francés* (or 'French road') in Spain. It has now been translated into English (see Appendix E).

Sunflower fields in the Gers

Routes to Santiago

The route described in this book is by no means the one and only 'Way of St James'. In former times, when pilgrims set out from their own front doors and made their way to Santiago from many different places, several well-established routes grew up (see map on page 6).

In France, for example, there were four main departure points, each with several 'feeder roads' (such as the one from Rocamadour to Moissac) joining them at different points along the way. The route from Paris, the *Via Turonensis*, passed through Orléans, Tours, Poitiers, Bordeaux and Dax. From Vézelay pilgrims took the *Via Lemovicensis* through Limoges, Périgeux, Bazas and Mont-de-Marsan, while those from Le Puy took the *Via Podensis* and passed through Conques, Cahors, Moissac, Aire-sur-l'Adour and Navarrenx.

All three routes joined up near Ostabat on the French side of the Pyrenees, to continue over the mountains to Roncesvalles and on across the north of Spain as the *Camino Francés*. The fourth way, from Arles, and known as the *Via Tolosana*, visited Saint-Gilles du Gard, Toulouse, Auch and Oloron but crossed the Pyrenees further east at the Col de Somport, from where it is known as the *Camino Aragonés*, before merging with the other three routes at Puenta la Reina.

Although the name *Camino de Santiago* has nowadays become more or less synonomous with the *Camino Francés* in Spain there were other important routes there too. These included the northern one along the Costa Cantabrica, the one taken by those English pilgrims who went by ship as far as Bordeaux and then continued on foot, while others sailed to La Coruña and then walked the rest of the way along one of the *Rutas del Mar*, one of which was known as the *Camino Inglés*. The *Vía de la Plata* or *Camino Mozárabe*, on the other hand, was the road taken by pilgrims from the south of Spain and others joining it by sea in Seville, passing through Mérida, Cáceres, Salamanca and Zamora before joining the *Camino Francés* at Astorga.

There were also routes from the east coast of Spain and two *caminos*, south to north, through Portugal, one inland, the other along the coast, as well as a whole network of routes reaching France from Austria, Switzerland, Italy, Germany, the Netherlands and countries much further afield.

What this guide covers

The 'Way of St James' described here corresponds to only a very small part of this complex web, to the section known as the *Via Podensis*, waymarked since the 1970s as the GR65. One of the most widely used nowadays and best-documented of the many pilgrim roads through France, it begins in Le Puy-en-Velay and passes through Conques, Figeac, Cahors, Moissac, Aire-sur-l'Adour and Saint Jean-Pied-de-Port.

The route description in this guide therefore begins in Le Puy-en-Velay, following the GR65 and continues through southern and south-western France to Saint-Jean-Pied-de-Port. The Spanish section of the route is covered in Cicerone's companion volume: *The Way of St James (Camino de Santiago): Pyrenees–Santiago–Finisterre*).

If you wish to break your journey into two, and would prefer to cross the Pyrenees at the end of your French walk (when you are fittest) rather than at the start of your Spanish journey, this guide also includes details of the route from Saint-Jean-Pied-de-Port to Roncevalles (and Pamplona) (two to three days more, and well served by public transport) as Appendix A.

This is followed by an outline of the three to four-day route from Saint-Palais direct to Irún (Appendix B), a new feature in this guide and an option not yet covered in any other guidebook. This option allows the pilgrim who prefers to continue on the *Camino del Norte* in Spain to do so, following the coastal route instead of the frequently over-populated *Camino Francés*, and is becoming increasingly popular. Instead of continuing directly south to Saint Jean-Pied-de-Port and over the Pyrenees to Roncesvalles, the pilgrim turns south-west and picks up the *Camino del Norte* at its starting point by the international bridge over the Río Bidasoa in Irún, the border between France and Spain.

Appendix C contains a suggestion for yet another option, the *variante* along the valley of the Célé. Appendix D lists St James's and other pilgrim references along the way, another feature not found in any other guides to this route. Also included are suggestions for further reading (Appendix E), a list of useful addresses and websites (Appendix F) and a glossary of geographical and other frequently encountered terms (Appendix G). Appendices H, I and J contain, respectively, an index of principal place names, an index of maps and a summary of the route with distances.

Anyone in Britain who is thinking of walking, cycling or riding any part of the route should contact the Confraternity of St James for advice and membership (see Appendix F for the address). The walker's route described here is not suitable for cyclists, however. Anyone wishing to tackle the route by road bike should get hold of John Higginson's *Way of St James: Le Puy to Santiago – A Cyclist's Guide* (2005), also published by Cicerone.

TOPOGRAPHY, ECONOMY AND LANGUAGE

The *Vía Podensis* begins in Le Puy-en-Velay in the *département* of the Haute-Loire and on the south-eastern edge of the Auvergne, a town famous for its bobbin-lace industry, its brown lentils and for being a pilgrimage centre in its own right (see page 43). The Velay is a volcanic region, its often barren landscape punctuated by innumerable *puys* (tall conical hills, derived from Latin *podium*) and latticed with ancient tracks and lanes frequently marked with old wayside

crosses. From here the route makes its way across the Margeride plateau and through the Gévaudan, an area best known for the mysterious wild beast (*la bête du Gévaudan*) that claimed so many lives towards the end of the 18th century.

After that, continuing to climb, it eases its way up onto the even higher open plateau land of the Aubrac, with its *drailles* (wide drove roads), its *burons* (shepherds' bothies) and its lush green meadows rising to nearly 4000ft. Flocks were driven up from the valleys below every year to spend the summer months grazing there, an activity known as *transhumance*. Pastors, each with several hundred animals, would make their way there on foot, a journey often lasting several days. Today this task is normally carried out in motorised vehicles, although an attempt has been made to revive the tradition; the tall wooden statue of a pastor in the village of Aubrac marks the first such expedition in 1990. This area is also famous for its *aligot*, a very substantial dish made of cheese and mashed potatoes.

After the Aubrac the landscape changes dramatically. The route continues down through the deep wooded gorges of the Lot valley and along the river itself to Estaing, before climbing up again and then plunging down into Conques (the name itself means 'small valley'), deep in the recesses of the hills. By this time the GR65 has reached the old region of the Rouergue. After emerging from

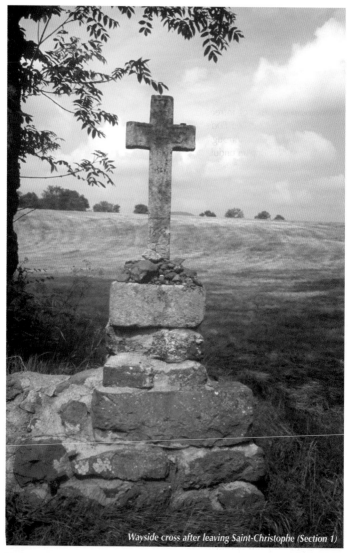

Wayside cross after leaving Saint-Christophe (Section 1)

here the countryside begins to open out again, before continuing through the chalky wooded area of the Quercy with its traditonal dovecotes (*pigeonniers*), its half-timbered houses, its *caselles* and *gaviotes* (small round hut-like buildings of drystone wall construction) and its not infrequent dolmens. After that the *Vía Podensis* makes its way to Cahors through the *causse*, a term denoting an undulating limestone plateau covered with scrubby vegetation, little water and few distinguishing features.

By now the observant pilgrim will have noted the many Occitan terms used in place names along the way: *mas, borie, couderc*, for example (see glossary in Appendix G), a language (not a dialect) of Latin origin. Historically France was divided into two main sections linguistically, the northern half with its *langue d'oïl*, the south with its *langue d'oc*, each quite separate languages and so-named because of their respective terms for the word 'yes'.

Occitan (often referred to as 'Provençal' as well) has an extensive literature from the Middle Ages and later, and was the only language spoken throughout the whole of the south of what we now know as France. But because the northern *langue d'oïl* was the one used in the royal court and because administrative power was increasingly centred in Paris, this became the official 'French' language spoken today. Occitan is still used by older people in country districts, but there are probably few speakers left in the early 21st century for whom it is their mother tongue. In recent decades there has been a revival of interest in the language, and as well as the emergence of modern authors writing in Occitan it can now be taught in schools and taken as a subsidiary subject both in the *baccalauréat* and at university level, as can Basque and Breton in other areas of France. Occitan also has several dialects, Béarnais and Gascon being those the pilgrim will encounter in toponomy along the Way of St James (*luy, gave*, for example – see Appendix G).

After Cahors the countryside gradually flattens out, beginning with the rolling landscapes of the *département* of the Tarn et Garonne and then, after crossing the Garonne itself near Moissac, on through the Gers (the least wooded *département* in France), with its rural bullrings, castles and *bastides* (small fortified towns) perched on hilltops, punctuating the vast undulating fields of corn, sunflowers and other crops. This is the old Armagnac region, famous for its brandy, after which the pilgrim goes on into the *département* of the Landes near Aire sur-l'Adour.

Here the landscape is almost completely flat arable land and the scenery is unremarkable. Its large-scale agriculture is the consequence of the *remembrement* of recent decades, the regrouping of small, uneconomic portions of land into larger, more viable units resulting in huge geometrically laid out fields with irrigation channels and few hedge boundaries. Then, slowly, the terrain becomes hillier again as the pilgrim passes through the Béarn, once a separate kingdom, before the route makes its way towards the foothills of the Pyrenees and the Basque country.

The Basque country as a geographical entity (as opposed to the present-day Spanish autonomous *región* of the *País vasco*) flanks both sides of the Pyrenees, three of its provinces lying in France (Laborde, Soule and Basse-Navarre), the other four in Spain (Alava, Guipúzcoa, Navarra and Viscaya). As you approach Saint-Jean-le-Vieux and Saint-Jean-Pied-de-Port you will begin to notice features that you will also encounter well into Spain, such as a changing local architecture; the large Basque houses with their overhanging eaves, often ornately decorated, and outside staircases and balconies running the whole length of one or more sides of the building are common, as is also the *frontón* or pelota court, to be found in almost every village of any size.

The Basque language (*Euskerra* in Basque) is unrelated to any of the Romance languages and its origins are still the subject of scholarly debate. It was formerly much more in evidence in the Basque provinces in Spain – whether in ordinary conversation, on television or on signs and notices – than it was on the French side, but since the late 1990s Basque has been used on bilingual road signs there too. With your arrival in this part of France in the foothills of the Pyrenees begins the transition to the Way of St James in Spain.

Vernacular architecture

Along the way you will see not only many interesting cathedrals, churches and other monuments of outstanding scale, character and significance but also examples of what is best described as 'vernacular architecture': wayside crosses, old bridges, *lavoirs* (communal laundry facilities), water mills, *métiers à ferrer les boeufs* (a device for immobilising oxen while they were being shod for work in the fields), *caselles, gaviotes* (different types of small, circular drystone buildings to protect shepherds and other workers from the elements), dovecotes and so on. Such features are indicated in the guide as you go along.

BEFORE YOU GO

- Read up as much as you can about the Way – its history, art, architecture and geography – as well as other people's accounts of their journeys. Suggestions for further reading are given in Appendix E.
- If you are not already used to walking or used to carrying a rucksack day in, day out, get in plenty of practice before you go. Consider joining your local rambling club at least six months in advance and go out with them as often as you can. Most clubs have walks of different lengths and speeds so you can start with a shorter, slower one if you need to and gradually build up your

speed and stamina. In this way you can benefit from walking with other people (usually friendly), walk in the countryside, have someone to lead who knows the way and suitable places to go (which you may not) and you can also practise walking in hilly places (which you will need).

- Then start increasing the amount of weight and luggage you take out with you until you can carry what you need. After that go out walking on at least two consecutive days on several occasions, in hilly places, carrying all your proposed gear with you: walking 30km on a 'one-off' basis is a very different matter from getting up again the following morning, probably stiff and possibly footsore, and starting out all over again. In this way you should have an enjoyable journey, with trouble-free feet and back.

- Don't expect anybody at all to speak English! Assume you will have to speak French all the time for everything you need, however complicated. So if you are not already fairly fluent, consider a year's evening classes or home study with tapes in your preparations; you will find yourself extremely isolated if you are unable not only to carry out practical transactions but also to converse with the many French-speaking pilgrims and other people you meet along the Way.

- Decide what type of footwear you will be taking – walking shoes, lightweight boots, heavy (thick-soled) trainers and so on – and break them in well before you go.

COMPANIONS

Two-legged Unless you plan to go with someone you already know well and have walked with before (family member or long-standing friend) think very carefully about your choice of companion, especially if you feel that you must go with someone else and better anybody at all than nobody. This area can be an absolute minefield and the following, in no particular order, are a few things to think about beforehand, rather than discover too late that they will cause problems. Some aspects are obvious: does the other person walk at the same speed as you, for example, or do the same sort of daily distances? Others are less so, however.

- If you do both walk at the same speed, does the other person like to continue non-stop until reaching a destination, only pausing for a quick drink or snack or like to sit down and admire the view as and when a suitable place appears?
- Do you (or your potential companion) like to
  - get up at dawn and start immediately while the other finds it difficult to get going in the morning? (Dittto early/late nights.)

- stay in hotels while the other person prefers to stay in gîtes d'étape or other economical accommodation?
- eat out in restaurants all the time while the other person wants to do his/her own cooking in gîtes/campsites?

- Does one of you speak fluent French while the other one is monolingual English? While it may be convenient for the non-French speaker to have a companion who can cope with all things practical, linguistically it can be frustrating for both of you when, for example, you get talking to other pilgrims or people who live along the way as either the French-speaker has to translate constantly or the other person is completely excluded from the conversation.

- Does one or the other of you talk non-stop while the other prefers to walk mainly in silence?

- Does one of you (but not the other) like to pause and visit churches and other monuments along the way?

- Do you both – something that is often overlooked until it is too late – both have the same level of funds available?

If walking speed, rhythm and rests are the only problem you can often resolve these by walking separately during the day and meeting in the evening (with plenty to talk about). Other issues are more difficult to resolve but they can make or mar a pilgrim journey in the constant company of another person.

Four-legged

Do not be tempted to take your dog with you.

- You will meet other, local dogs along the way who are on their own territory and do not take kindly to strange ones.
- Hardly any accommodation of any type, except campsites, accepts them. On accommodation lists places routinely say 'chiens refusés'.
- You may well have transport problems returning home, especially in Spain.
- Most dogs, although used to going out all day long, are not accustomed to continuous long-distance walking and, like their two-legged companions, are prone to problems with their feet.

PLANNING YOUR SCHEDULE

The walk from Le Puy to Saint-Jean-Pied-de-Port can be completed in four to five weeks by anyone who is fairly fit and who also likes to visit places of interest along the way. It can be undertaken in sections, too, by those who lack the time to do it all in one go or who would just like to cover certain stretches, and indications are given in the text as to how to reach (or leave) the main towns along the Way.

Allow plenty of time when planning your itinerary, especially if you are not an experienced walker. Start with fairly short stages and always stop before you are tired. You can increase the distances as you get fitter and into the swing of things. Try not to plan too tight a schedule either, but allow plenty of time and flexibility to account for unforeseen circumstances (pleasant or otherwise).

Where and how many rest days you take is up to you (though Conques, Cahors and Moissac are 'musts'), as is whether you include several short days' walking in your programme, arriving at your destination during the late morning so

as to have the remainder of the day completely free. If you are extremely tired or having trouble with your feet, a complete day off works wonders (particularly in a small place with no 'sights' to be visited) and is well worth the disruption to your schedule that it might initially seem to be.

If you are walking all the way to Santiago in one go consider taking a day off in Saint-Jean-Pied-de-Port as you leave the French section of the route behind you and set out on the next (much easier physically, once you have crossed the Pyrenees) part of the route through Spain.

Métier à ferrer les boeufs, Rieutort d'Aubrac (Section 1)

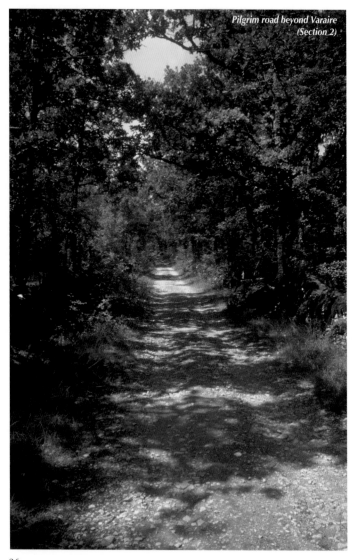

Pilgrim road beyond Varaire
(Section 2)

EQUIPMENT

Rucksack At least 50 litres in capacity if carrying a sleeping bag

Footwear Both to walk in and a spare pair of lightweight trainers/sandals

Waterproofs Even in summer it may rain, especially in the Basque country. A poncho (a cape with a hood and space inside for a rucksack) is far more useful (and far less hot) than a cagoule or anorak

Pullover or fleece jacket Parts of the route are high up and it can get cold at night, even in summer

First aid kit Include a needle for draining blisters and scissors. The type of plaster sold by the metre is more useful than individual dressings. Also high-factor sunscreen if you burn easily. Insect repellant in July and August

Torch

Large water bottle At least 2 litres in capacity if walking in July and August

Sleeping bag Essential if you are either camping or continuing into Spain and will be staying in *refugios* there, but if you are only doing the French section and are staying in gîtes d'étape a **sheet sleeping bag** will normally be sufficient as blankets are usually provided

Thin pillowcase Useful in gîtes (or tent) to hold clothes when pillows are not provided

Sleeping mat If camping

Stick Useful for fending off/frightening dogs and testing boggy terrain

Guidebook and maps

Compass

Sun hat Preferably with wide brim

Small dictionary

Mug, spoon, plate and knife

A **tent** is useful if you intend to camp a lot (though you can walk the entire route from Le Puy to the Pyrenees staying in gîtes); in this case you will also need a 'camping gaz' type stove or similar. In general, travel as light as you can, not just for the weight but because of the constant hills and, depending on the season, the heat.

GETTING THERE AND BACK

Le Puy By train from Paris (Gare de Lyon) to Saint-Etienne by TGV and then by local train; by coach direct from London to Lyon (Fridays, summer only) and then by local train via Saint-Etienne; by plane to Lyon and then by local train via Saint-Etienne

Aumont-Aubrac By train from Paris (Austerlitz) to Figeac (Gare) and then by bus

Cahors By train from Paris (Austerlitz on the Toulouse service); by coach from London (on the Toulouse service, Mondays and Fridays, summer only, change in Lille and Tours); by plane to Limoges (from London Stansted, East Midlands Airport, for example) and then by train

Decazeville and **Figeac** are accessible by train from Paris (Austerlitz)

Moissac By train from Paris (via Bordeaux or Toulouse)

Aire sur l'Adour By train from Paris (Austerlitz) to Dax and then by bus

Orthez By train from Paris (Austerlitz)

Saint-Jean-Pied-de-Port By local train to Bayonne and then to Paris

(Austerlitz) by TGV; by coach to London (Wednesdays and Sundays, summer only, change in Tours and Lille). Ryanair has flights to London Stansted from Biarritz (close to Bayonne and therefore accessible by train from Saint-Jean Pied-de-Port for the return journey)

Roncevalles (or Pamplona) (if crossing the Pyrenees to finish the French section of your journey there) By train or coach from Madrid; coach from Bilbao.

However, as coach and budget airline services are particularly subject to change it is advisable to check this information well before planning your journey. NB: the easiest way to check on train services in France is often on the website of the German(!) railways: www.bahn.de (then click on the sign to get the information in English).

ACCOMMODATION

There are four broad types of accommodation available along the route: campsites, *gîtes d'étape, chambres d'hôte* and hotels, alongside the slowly developing network of *Accueils Chrétiens*.

Most towns, even small, and especially those on a river, have a campsite, and many farms along the way offer *camping à la ferme*. Campsites vary in price according to the facilities they offer, but as more and more sites are being upgraded it may now be very little cheaper to camp than to stay in a *gîte d'étape* (see below). The only real advantage in carrying a tent

is the freedom to stop when and where you want as campsites are so numerous. Most are closed in winter (from *Toussaint* – All Saints Day, a public holiday on 1 November – to Easter) but opening times, where known, are indicated in the text. Note, however, that several of the larger campsites have caravans or mobile homes that they rent out to pilgrims per person per night, normally with cooking facilities too (Livinhac le Haut, Aire-sur-l'Adour, for example) so if you are having difficulty finding somewhere to sleep this is an option worth checking out.

It is also possible to walk the entire route from Le Puy to the Pyrenees staying in gîtes d'étape, and without having to cover enormous distances between stops. These contain simple, dormitory-type accommodation and at least one hot shower, and the municipally-run ones at least offer cooking facilities (these are indicated with a K in the text). In 2009 they cost between €8 and €14 per person per night. Blankets are usually provided so normally only a sheet sleeping bag is needed. Most include special clothes-washing sinks and, increasingly, a washing machine for a small fee.

The gîtes d'étape (as opposed to other types of gîte) are for walkers, cyclists and riders only; there are now plenty within easy walking distance of each other (every 15km or so) as far as Conques, but after that they are often further apart (around 20-25km). Many are municipally run (*gîte communal*) and will contain all the above facilities,

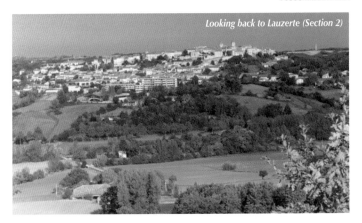

Looking back to Lauzerte (Section 2)

but in some places establishments that describe themselves as gîtes d'étape provide no cooking facilities and few opportunities, for example, to wash clothes. These are often run by restaurants, hotels, riding schools or bed and breakfast establishments that attach a dormitory and showers and provide meals, usually with a *soirée étape* or *forfait pèlerin* (ie a special rate for dinner, bed and breakfast) which, pilgrims report increasingly, may be a pre-condition of staying there. So be on your guard and check carefully before making a reservation, especially if you are on a tight budget. This type of gîte is also, usually, more expensive than the municipally run ones.

In popular areas it is advisable to phone the day before, especially at holiday times or on weekends with a *pont* (a public holiday on a Thursday or a Tuesday when people take Friday or Monday off as well) as walking clubs and other groups sometimes book (and pay for) the whole gîte, even if they do not always fill it. In such cases it is usually possible to sleep there once you are actually on the spot, but good French will be needed to negotiate. (Unlike the *refugios* in Spain, they do not let people sleep on the floor when the normal sleeping facilities are full.) *Gîtes d'étape* may seem too spartan for some people's tastes, but they are a very good way to meet and get to know other pilgrims, as are the *refugios* in Spain, especially if you are walking or cycling the entire route. Many, like the campsites, are only open from Easter to October, but information regarding their availability is given where known.

Those who prefer to stay in *chambres d'hôte* (abbreviated to 'CH' here), the French equivalent of bed and breakfast in country areas and usually offering

29

an evening meal as well, will also have no trouble as these establishments are becoming increasingly popular. It is usually enough to phone a day or so ahead, but given the proliferation of these facilities and the fact that many of them only offer one or two rooms, contact details have only been given in this text when there are only one or two such offerings in the place concerned; where the supply is plentiful you can either contact the tourist office (TO) in question or consult the *Miam Miam Dodo* guide (see below).

The word *hôtel* in France covers everything from luxurious four-star accommodation (France does not have hotels classified with five stars) to a very basic *pension* or *hôtel de préfecture*, and their prices normally reflect the facilities available. French hotels are currently being reclassified, however, and those that have already been done usually have 'NN' (*nouveaux normes*) after their star rating. If you prefer to stay in hotels you will find the local *Pages Jaunes* (Yellow Pages), available in most cafés, useful for accommodation (particularly the lower end of the market), although the entries in the *Miam Miam Dodo* guide (see below) are very comprehensive. A hotel offering a *forfait pèlerin* (or *soirée étape*) has, like other establishments, a special rate for dinner, bed and breakfast.

Gradually, however, a fifth category of accommodation, strictly for pilgrims only (a *créanciale* – pilgrim passport, see below – is necessary to access them), is beginning to establish itself on the Le Puy route, often described as *Accueils Chrétiens*. These provide dormitory-type accommodation, offer a shared meal in the evening and breakfast the following morning and sometimes the opportunity for evening prayers and, like the refugio system in Spain, operate on a donation (*libre participation*) basis. Their availability is also indicated in the relevant sections of this guide.

Do not confuse these, however, with the *Accueil Pèlerins*, a service offered (usually from Easter to October) by volunteers, often former pilgrims, from an increasing number of churches and local pilgrim associations; this provides the passing pilgrim with information, a cold drink or coffee and the chance to have their pilgrim passport stamped. (These are abbreviated in the text as AP.)

As well as the information given in this guide, another source of very up-to-date information is highly recommended to accompany this book, for all types of accommodation (including hotels) and services (shops, restaurants, banks, internet facilities and so on) and is revised and reprinted annually (make sure you get the GR65 Le Puy edition) – the somewhat curiously entitled *Miam Miam Dodo*. Lauriane and Jacques Clouteau, *Miam Miam Dodo, Le Chemin de Saint Jacques de Compostelle: la Voie du Puy*, Les Editions du Vieux Crayon, is an extremely detailed guide to where to sleep and eat along the way (its title translates something like 'Yum-Yum-Byebyes') and although it is in French its schematic presentation makes it very easy to use, even for those with limited knowledge of the language. It also lists facilities within a 5km radius of places on the route. It is available direct from its authors (see Appendix F), from the Confraternity of St James's online bookshop, from the cathedral and other bookshops in Le Puy and in other places along the route as well as in some gîtes d'étape.

PLANNING THE DAY

Long-distance walkers in Britain usually operate on a 'nine-to-five' basis, leaving their accommodation shortly after breakfast and returning in time for an early evening meal. There may be few, if any, places of historical, religious or cultural interest, such as churches, cathedrals or stately homes, directly on the path that require a detailed indoor visit (as opposed to historic bridges, fortifications, market crosses and so on that can be inspected fairly quickly from the outside), and those that do normally work 'nine-to-five' as well so that combining walking and sightseeing is usually incompatible. Therefore, walkers in Britain tend just to walk.

In France, however, not only are there an enormous number of places well worth visiting along the Le Puy route, of outstanding artistic, architectural, cultural or religious interest, but they are also open at convenient times for the walker: as well as 10:00 to

Pilgrim road in the Lot (Section 2)

31

Chapelle Sainte-Foy (Section 1)

12:00 they normally open again in the evenings from 16:00 or 17:00 to 19:00. Churches in the *départements* of the Haute Loire, Lozère, Aveyron, Lot, Tarn et Garonne, Gers and the Landes are usually open all day long from April to October, but in the Pyrénées Orienales those in small villages were almost always firmly locked in summer 2009 (when this guide was being prepared) unless a service was going on.

In July and August in particular it is extremely hot during the day, particularly in the *causse* before Cahors, with temperatures well up into the 90°sF, although in many areas there is often a lot of shade. When walking in hot weather it is important to avoid becoming dehydrated by drinking plenty of water before you set out; once you realise you haven't had enough to drink it is too late to do anything about it, even if you have supplies with you (top up your water bottle whenever you can).

It is difficult to do but if you can drink *at* least half a litre of water as soon as you get up (as well as any tea/coffee available) you will find the hot weather affects you much less. The best way to avoid walking in the heat is to get up before it is light and set out at daybreak. At this time of day it is cool and pleasant, with the added advantages of watching the sun rise as you walk and enjoying the scenery in the early morning light.

In this way, even with stops, you should be able to reach your destination by the early afternoon, when you can then rest up awhile before going out sightseeing or visiting in the (relative) cool of the early evening. It is also a good idea, in large towns and other places of any size, to go for a walk in the evening and check your route out, so as not to waste time or get lost the following morning.

OTHER PRACTICAL INFORMATION

Shops Shops (for food) are open until 12:00 or 12:30, and then from 14:30 or 15:00 until about 19:00. Those in small villages (where they still exist) are usually shut not only on Sundays but often on Monday mornings (and sometimes afternoons) as well, so considerable organisation is needed when following the GR65, particularly if you are doing your own cooking.

Public holidays There are more of these in France (*jours fériés*) than in Britain: 1 January, 1 and 8 May, Ascension Day, 14 July, 15 August, 1 November, and 11 and 25 December. Shops, including those for food (but not bars, restaurants or bakeries) will be closed on these occasions.

Meals In France meals are available between 12:00 and 14:00 and from 19:00 to 21:00. (If you are a vegetarian you will probably find eating out very difficult.) Breakfast (in hotels and so on) is usually available from 07:00 or 07:30 onwards. **Cafés and bars** may open as early as 0700 in summer along the pilgrim route (check first if you want breakfast before setting out) and may well close by 22:00 in large towns and much earlier in small places.

Changing money It is usually possible to change money in post offices in France, even in quite small places. There is also an increasing number of cashpoints (*distributeurs de billets de banque*, ATMS in the text), even in fairly small towns, which accept Visa, cash cards bearing the Cirrus/Maestro logo, and so on. Banks' opening hours are similar to those in Britain.

Post offices These (the 'PTT') are open from 08:00 in large places, 09:00 in small and until as late as 19:00 (12:30 or 13:00 on Saturdays) and many of them have cashpoints too. If you want to send things to yourself further along the route (such as maps and guides) or have people write to you, you can do this via the *poste restante* system whereby you collect your mail (on presentation of your passport) at the post office. Address the letter or parcel to yourself (surname first), Poste Restante, postal code and name of town. The most likely places you will need will be the following: 43000 Le Puy-en-Velay, 46100 Figeac, 46000 Cahors, 82200 Moissac, 40800 Aire sur l'Adour and 64220 Saint-Jean-Pied-de-Port. There is a small fee for each item collected and they only keep them for 15 days before returning them to the sender.

Telephones Most public telephones operate with *télécartes* (phone cards), except in rural areas. All phone numbers in France consist of 10 digits, with 01, 02, 03, 04 or 05 placed at the start of the previously eight-figure numbers, according to the region they are in (06 is reserved for mobile phones). (Note that if you phone from Britain you do not use the '0'.) The emergency number in France for all services is now 112.

As **mobile phones** frequently do not work in rural areas, and as there are still plenty of telephone boxes *(cabines téléphoniques)* or *points-phones* along the route, it might be better to leave your mobile at home or keep it strictly for emergencies. You will also find it a much more 'pilgrim' journey if your friends and relations back home cannot contact you (rather than you ringing them) to tell you, for example, that the central heating doesn't work, that the cat next door has been run over or that your mother-in-law has broken her spectacles...

Internet/Cybercafés These are not nearly as easy to find in France as they are on the Spanish section of the route and as their availability changes frequently they have not been listed in this guide. However, they are indicated in *Miam Miam Dodo* and TOs can usually tell you where to find one.

Launderettes These can be found in all large French towns (unlike Spain, where they do not exist) and, as indicated above, many gîtes d'étape now have washing machines.

Buvettes or **pauses-café** Stalls/places selling drinks and snacks and sometimes local produce as well, are increasingly available along this route, often run by farms or by local people, particularly in isolated areas. You can also eat your own food there, provided you buy a drink. They are not listed in this guide as their availability changes frequently but their enterprising owners normally post notices well in advance to alert you to their existence.

Drinking water There are many places along the way with a *point d'eau*, either taps or fountains, and marked 'eau potable' when it is safe to drink. These are indicated in the text with a ♣ symbol. There are also many public WCs, particularly in small places, often in or near the *mairie* (town hall).

Stamps for pilgrim passports Modern pilgrims who seek proof of their pilgrimage also carry a 'pilgrim passport' (*créanciale* in French) which they have stamped at regular intervals along the Way (in churches, TOs, town halls and many gîtes d'étape) and which they then present to the Cathedral authorities in Santiago to help them

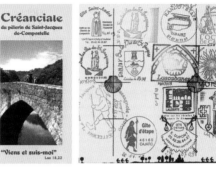

Above left: Créanciale (pilgrim passport) issued by the Eglise de France
Above right: Stamps in a pilgrim passport

obtain their *Compostela* (certificate of completion of pilgrimage). More information about 'pilgrim passports' is available (to its members) from the Confraternity of St James but the *Créanciale* itself issued by the Eglise de France, is available (in person only) from the Cathedral in Le Puy when you arrive there.

Church services Although most churches are open all day, as explained above, apart from in large towns there is often only a mass there once a fortnight, or once a month in really small places. A list of mass times and where they will be held in the local area is normally posted in churches for the current and following month.

Medical assistance Make sure that you obtain an **EHIC (European Health Insurance Card)** before leaving Britain (application forms are available from the post office). This is a Europe-wide document entitling you to free or reduced medical (but not dental) treatment under the French health system. If you already have one, check its expiry date before departure. Note, however, that the EHIC does not cover transport home, for which you will need separate insurance. If you wear glasses all the time take either a spare pair or the prescription with you.

Snakes have been seen recently on the stretch from Le Puy to Cahors, and also between Saint-Palais and Saint-Jean-Pied-de-Port. They may not be very common but if you do meet them (usually when it has been very hot for a while) it will be when you are off your guard (stick useful).

Hunting season When this opens (1 October onwards) be particularly vigilant when walking through forests and stick to the paths, especially at weekends and on public holidays when pheasant shooting and other game hunting is extremely popular.

Dogs Their owners nearly always tell you, 'he won't hurt you' ('il n'est pas méchant') but this is often hard to believe. They may tell you, too, that it is the rucksack that bothers them (and as dogs are reputed to see only in black and white there may be some truth in this, faced with mysterious hump-backed monsters on two legs) but it is not much comfort when faced with an aggressive one. They live all along the route from Le Puy to the Pyrenees (as well as on the Spanish section of the route), are often (but not always) tied up, hear you ages before you have any idea where they are and are often enormous. (The small ones are, in fact, a greater nuisance, as they have a nasty habit of letting you pass quietly by and then attacking from behind, nipping you in the back of your ankles.) A **stick** is very useful – even though you might not usually walk with one – not to hit them with, but to threaten. Be warned!

Baggage transfer services A number of hotels and *chambres d'hôte* proprietors now offer to transport your luggage to the next overnight stop for you, either free or for a small fee (where this is the case it is indicated after each entry in the *Miam Miam Dodo* guide). However, there are also several firms operating a service of this type along the entire route from Le Puy to Saint-Jean-Pied-de-Port on a regular basis, with the option of returning you to your starting point eastwards (if you are only doing a section) when they return empty after delivering the day's bags.

Details of companies offering such 'sherpa' services are given in Appendix F. (In 2009 the standard charge was €8 per item per stage, with a maximum of 12 kilos per bag.) It is recommended, however, that you carry your own luggage wherever possible as you will find it a much more pilgrim (as opposed to holiday) experience and only resort to such services in emergencies.

USING THIS GUIDE

Waymarking

The route described in this book follows the GR65 through France, ending at the border town of Saint-Jean-Pied-de-Port, in the direction of the (modern) pilgrimage. It is described in one direction only. Those who would like to walk the Way in reverse or return on foot will have no trouble in France as the route (unlike in Spain) is waymarked in both directions. Waymarking (*balisage*) is in the form of pairs of horizontal red-and-white stripes (*balises*), one above the other to indicate that you should continue ahead (see diagram, right). Turns are indicated by bent red-and-white arrows, often preceded by broken waymarks to prepare the walker.

A useful feature is also the 'wrong direction' sign, a red-and-white cross telling you which direction not to take, especially in situations where it is hard to mark the correct option for lack of suitable trees, rocks and so on, on which to paint them. If you wonder at times why information about other routes is given in the description of this route, it is because all French long-distance footpaths (the *Sentiers de Grandes Randonnées* or 'GRs') have the same waymarking system and you should be alert to (usually short) sections which the GR65 has in common with, for example, the GR4. When they separate again you need to know which turning is the correct one as there is not always an indication next to the waymark.

You will also see, however, increasingly frequently in the early stages of the route, the yellow arrows familiar to those who have already walked the *Camino* in Spain, the European shell logo on a blue background (often with the number of kilometres still remaining to Santiago) and, in the Landes and Pyrénées-Atlantiques, yellow stickers/markers with the blue shell motif.

Note, however, that the GR65 has not been waymarked with the long-distance pilgrim (as opposed to

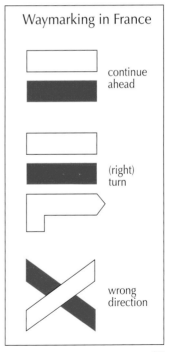

Waymarking in France

continue ahead

(right) turn

wrong direction

Pilgrim waymarking in Le Puy

holiday walker) in mind: that is, someone who is going to walk, if not all the way to Santiago in one go, then at least as far as Saint-Jean-Pied-de-Port, and thus wants to take the most direct route possible without walking on busy roads or missing essential monuments and places of interest. Instead the GR65 caters more for the needs of hikers or ramblers who are probably only doing a short section of the entire route or are just out for the day and thus have time to make 'scenic' detours in order simply to have good views, for example when approaching Saint-Côme-d'Olt.

The GR65 also goes to some lengths in places to make sure that the walker avoids tarmac at all costs, doing 'loops' that involve going round three sides of a square when a short section on a very minor road (with little or no traffic) would be much more direct, or up and down steep hills on tracks parallel to a road. Such places are indicated in the text with alternative strategies suggested, for instance in bad weather. It is therefore important to read through the description of the following day's walk ahead of time and decide which option you would like to take in such cases. The GR65

also studiously avoids shops and bars at times, making life difficult when you need to purchase food supplies, but again alternative tactics are suggested when available.

Maps

Michelin 725 is a single map covering the whole of southern France, but maps in the IGN (Institut Géographique National) new lime-green Top 100 *Tourisme et Découverte* series are recommended for walkers as the GR65 and its *variantes* are marked on them. The scale is 1:100,000 and only five are required (as against 25 in the blue 1:25,000 *Carte de Randonée* series) and are given here in route order: 156 (St-Etienne–Le Puy-en-Velay), 162 (Rodez–Millau), 161 (Montauban–Albi), 159 (Pau–Mont-de-Marsan) and 166 (Pau–Bayonne).

These are available from Stanfords map shop in London, from The Map Shop, Upton-upon-Severn or from many general bookshops but make sure you get the latest edition. However, at the time this edition was being prepared 156 (St Etienne–Le Puy-en-Velay) had not been published so until this is ready you will need to use No 50 (of the same title and on the same scale) in the former blue *Cartes de Promenade* series.

Users of previous editions of this guide have often asked why 'proper' Ordnance Survey-type maps are not provided in this book. Ideally the author would like them to be but problems of copyright and reprinting make it extremely complicated. Instead, to aid the pilgrim or walker in planning his or her journey, it has only been possible to include sketch maps of the route in this guide.

Textual description

The text is divided up into four sections, split at Figeac, Moissac and aire-sur-l'Adour: these are all places where the walker can reach or leave the route easily by public transport, if they wish to complete the route in shorter stages. Each of the main places along the route appears in **bold**, preceded by the distance walked from the previous place and followed by a description of the facilities available, a brief history where applicable and an indication of the places of interest to visit. (Walkers wishing to spend time in any of the larger towns should obtain information leaflets and a street plan from the TO there.)

The text is not divided up into stages, as in this way the walker can decide the distances he or she would like to cover each day. (It is suggested that you go through the text in advance and mark in possible overnight stops with a highlight pen.) The figures after each place name heading indicate the height in metres where known and, in parentheses, the distance in kilometres

Chapelle Saint-Roch, Montbonnet (Section 1)

from both Le Puy and Saint-Jean-Pied-de-Port. In the case of large towns (Cahors, for example) the distances to/from them start/end in their centres, normally at the cathedral.

Place names appear in the text in **bold type**, as do other names that help in wayfinding, such as street names, the names of prominent buildings, rivers and so on.

Abbreviations used in the text:
L indicates that you should turn/fork left; R that you should turn/fork R. (L) and (R) mean that something you pass is to your left or right. KSO = Keep Straight On. KSO(L) or KSO(R) = Keep Straight On L or R. FB = footbridge, FP = footpath, > = becomes, // = parallel. Km = kilometre. N followed by a number (such as N135) refers to the number of a main road, D to that of a local road. AP = Accueil Pèlerin, CH = Chambre d'Hôte, K = kitchen/cooking facilities. TO = tourist office, PTT = post office. RE = reservation essential. X = closed/except, ♣ = drinking water available. ATM = cash dispenser (ATM). SNCF is the abbreviation for the French national railway network. HT = High Tension (cables).

A comfortable pace
Unlike pilgrimages to Lourdes, Fatima or other locations where miracles are sought and help for specific problems requested, and where being in the pilgrim destination itself is the most important factor, on the Way of St James it is the journey that

40

is the pilgrim's principal concern, the arrival in Santiago being only a conclusion to the rest of the undertaking. It is not a 'map and compass route' either, although the walking along the Le Puy route is often strenuous. Timings have not been given from place to place, but 4km per hour, exclusive of stops, is often considered average, especially when carrying a heavy rucksack. However, a comfortable pace may often be more than this – a fit walker may well be able to maintain a speed of 5 to 6km or 3.5 miles per hour.

WHEN TO GO

The route is practicable, but not necessarily recommended, all through the year. In winter there is often snow on the Aubrac plateau and nearly always in the Pyrenees, and it rains a lot in the Basque country, something it does on all parts of the route in spring. If you are not restricted to a particular time of year then May or early June or the autumn are best – dry, but not as hot as in summer, but accommodation is naturally becoming increasingly crowded then.

Traditionally as many people as possible aimed to arrive in Santiago for the festivities on 25 July, St James's Day, particularly in Holy Years. Many people still do.

SECTION 1
Le Puy-en-Velay to Figeac

Le Puy-en-Velay 625m (0/738)

Population 29,000. All facilities. SNCF (trains from Paris via Saint-Etienne-Châteaucreux. Several hotels and CH (see *Miam Miam Dodo*). 3 gîtes d'étape: a) Le Relais du pèlerin Saint-Jacques, 28 Rue Cardinal de Polignac (near cathedral, 06.37.08.65.83), open 1 April to 31 October from 15:00 and run by former pilgrim volunteers from the Rhône-Alpes association, 43pl, pilgrims only, no fixed charge but donation; b) for pilgrims and walkers in the Maison Saint-François (also near cathedral, 04.71.05.98.86, 19pl, K), Rue Mayol, open all year; c) Gîte d'Etape des Capucins (and adjoining Appart'Hôtel) is on the route out of town at 29 Rue de Capucins (04.71.04.28.74 & 06.63.09.13.69, open all year, 19pl, K). Youth hostel (04.71.05.52.40, open all year but closed w/ends 31/10–31/3, 72pl, K) in Centre Pierre Cardinal, Rue Jules Vallès, also in the upper part of town, as is the Accueil Saint Georges, Grand Séminaire, 4 Rue Saint Georges, which also takes pilgrims (04.71.09.93.10, open all year, 200 pl but is often full with very large groups). Campsite (Camping municipal de Bouthezard), Chemin de Roderie, Rocade d'Aiguilhe, is to NW of town, on an island in the river (15/3–1/10).

Pilgrim stamp (and *créanciale* – pilgrim passport, if desired) available from the cathedral sacristy (10:00–12:00, 14:00–18:00 April to Sept, 10:00–12:00 and 15:00–17:00 at other times). Mass in cathedral at 07:00 every morning (conducted by the Bishop of Le Puy whenever possible), followed by pilgrim blessing (stamp also available then). The '*Amis du Puy*', many of them former pilgrims, hold an information session with a '*verre d'amitié*' (informal drink) every evening from 1/4–15/10, 18:00–19:30, at 29 Rue Cardinal de Polignac (in old part of town), where they also issue (and stamp) pilgrim passports.

Le Puy (its inhabitants are known as *ponot(e)s*) is an ancient town in a volcanic landscape, dominated by rocky peaks rising from the valley floor. One is crowned by the chapel of Saint Michel d'Aiguilhe (the Needle), built by Godescalc, Bishop of Le Puy, after his pilgrimage to Santiago in AD951 (it is worth climbing the 267 steps to visit it). An enormous statue of Notre-Dame de France overlooks the town from a rock high above. It is worth spending at

▶

St James as a pilgrim, Le Puy Cathedral (Photo: Marigold Fox)

least half a day visiting Le Puy. Ask at Office de Tourisme (Place du Clauzel) for a walking tour plan of the town. Musée Crozatier, Eglise du Collège, first 'Jesuit-style' church in France, 13th-century Eglise Saint-Laurent, Chapelle des Pénitents, Baptistère Saint-Jean, Chapel of Monastère Sainte-Claire, Tour Pannessac. Le Puy is also famous for its lentils and its bobbin-lace making. (If you are interested in the latter the Atelier Conservatoire National de la Dentelle du Puy-en-Velay, 36 Rue du 82e Reg. d'Infanterie – free of charge – is worth a visit.)

The Romanesque Cathedral of Notre-Dame (open 06:30–19:30 daily), now fully restored, is surrounded by the narrow twisting streets of the old town with many interesting houses. Inside the cathedral: 11th–12th-century cloisters and 17th-century statue of the Black Virgin, which was originally in the former Chapelle de St Maurice du refuge. This replaces a cedar statue from Egypt, brought back by King Louis IX (Saint Louis) after the seventh crusade but burnt by ultra-revolutionaries on Whitsunday 1794.

There are various theories as to the origins of the Black Virgins. Once considered to have come only from Coptic Africa they have also been thought to be local, and 'black' either because of a life of hard work in the fields and the open air or 'black' because of being sinful (Mary Magdalene would therefore fall into this category). Whatever the explanation, the black Virgin in Le Puy plays an important role in the life of the cathedral and possesses a complete liturgical 'wardrobe', changed, along with altar cloth, vestments, and so on, according to the seasons of the church's year.

Le Puy has been a pilgrimage centre since the Middle Ages, not so much, as is often thought, as a starting (or assembly) point for French pilgrims and the many 'feeder' routes and/or those coming from further afield en route to Santiago, but as a pilgrimage destination in its own right. Pilgrimages to Notre-Dame du Puy began in the 10th century and the shrine has its own 'Jubilee' years, those in which the Feast of the Annunciation (25 March) coincides with Good Friday. The first was in 992 (thus predating the first Holy Year in Santiago, in 1179) and is the third oldest after Jerusalem and Rome. There were three such Jubilee years in the 20th century – 1910, 1921 and 1932. The first one in the 21st century fell on 25 March 2005; the next one is in 2016 but the one after that is not until 2157. The Rue des Pèlerins and the Hôtel des Pèlerins were therefore not used initially by pilgrims to Santiago, as is often supposed, but by those on pilgrimage to the shrine of Notre-Dame du Puy.

Despite the fact that one of Le Puy's 16 town gates (many of which were named after a saint) was the Porte Sainct Jacme (from where pilgrims left to

▶

go to 'monseigneur Sainct Jacques le Majeur en Compostelle ou Galice') Le Puy's connection with the pilgrimage to Santiago de Compostela was not common knowledge until the 19th century when, after the departmental archives of the Haute-Loire were reopened and the innumerable documents confiscated during the French Revolution became available, it was discovered, for example, that Godescalc, Bishop of Le Puy, had made the pilgrimage to Santiago in 951. This was something only known to a small circle of erudite research workers, however, and there was no mention of the hordes of pilgrims Godescalc was supposed to have incited to follow in his footsteps. Inventories in these archives also revealed that in 1253 the town of Le Puy possessed several hospitals, dedicated to different saints including Saint James, while the first Latin translation of Aymery Picard's *Pilgrim Guide* in 1882 mentioned the town as one of the 'four historic routes' to Compostelle, passing through Conques and Moissac.

The popularity of Le Puy as a departure point for pilgrims bound for Santiago is, in fact, a mid-20th-century phenomenon, encouraged in part by one or two bishops interested in the subject but mainly by the creation of the GR65, a long-distance footpath established by the forerunners of the present FFRP (Fédération Française de la Randonée Pédestre, the French national walking organization) in the early 1970s to 'reinvent' a pilgrim route from that part of France. But although the *Via Podensis* or route from Le Puy-en-Velay was mentioned as one of the four main departure points in France in Aymery Picard's guide (see above) it was much less travelled in the past than the Paris/Tours, Vézelay and Arles routes (nowadays the reverse is true) and with much fewer pilgrim-related monuments and associations.

The idea at the time, as recreational walking began to become popular in France, was to create a route through wonderful scenery (the Velay region, the Aubrac, the Margeride…), avoiding towns at all costs, as well as roads with a lot of traffic (even if they were historically appropriate), passing as many places with Jacobean and other pilgrim references (St Roch chapels, for example) as possible and opting for a route where accommodation was available. The result was a scenic long-distance footpath, far from direct, with a lot of detours, that addresses the needs of walkers with plenty of time to spare, rather than pilgrims who need the most direct, safe and traffic-free route to a final desination many hundreds of kilometers away. The GR65 has become increasingly popular all the same, not only as a starting-point for those beginning the pilgrimage in France but also as an interim halt for those coming from Geneva on its extension from there, from other parts of Switzerland, from Germany and beyond.

Map 1: Le Puy-en-Velay to Roziers

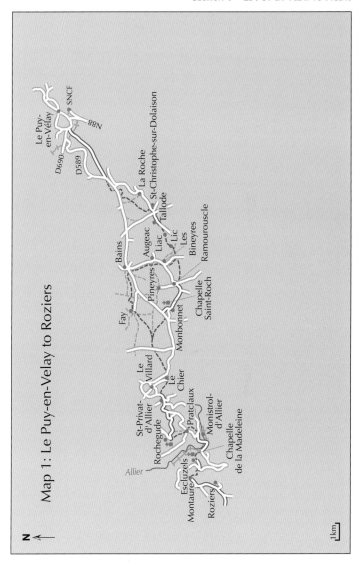

N ←

Le Puy-en-Vélay

SNCF

N88

D690

D589

La Roche

St-Christophe-sur-Dolaison

Tallode

Bains

Augeac

Liac

Lic

Les Bineyres

Ramourouscle

Pineyres

Chapelle Saint-Roch

Fay

Monbonnet

St-Privat-d'Allier

Le Villard

Le Chier

Rochegude

Pratclaux

Monistrol-d'Allier

Chapelle de la Madeleine

Allier

Escluzels

Montaure

Roziers

1km

When planning your first day remember that from Le Puy (625mn) to the Lac d'Oeuf (1206m) the 20km stretch between Montbonnet and Saint-Privat-d'Allier is continuously uphill.

Starting from the inside of the cathedral and with your back to the main altar *(note statue of St James the pilgrim on pillar to LH side of aisle, facing altar – this dates from the 15th century but was only purchased for the cathedral, by public subscription, in 1990)* go down the main staircase ahead. Go down the long flight of steps outside and then down the **Rue des Tables** ahead *(note old houses with statues in niches at first-floor level)*. Turn L after the fountain (des 'Choristes') into the **Rue Raphaël**. KSO to the end and continue, veering R, down **Rue Chènebouterie** to the **Place du Plot**, the traditional pilgrim starting point. Turn R at end into the **Rue Saint-Jacques** *(statue of St James the pilgrim in niche above chemist's shop on corner of this street and the Place du Plot, plaque of 'Amis de Saint-Jacques' on wall on L)*. Cross **Boulevard Saint-Louis** and KSO uphill, climbing steeply *(several benches en route)*, up the **Rue des Capucins**. At the top there is the first clear waymark and large wooden statue of St James pilgrim on L: turn R and then L after 50m up the **Route de Compostelle**, continuing to climb steadily. KSO(L) at fork and at bend in road turn R up FP by sports field and then L up a flight of steps back up to the road, where you turn R. *(Handy seat at top, positioned with a good view back over Le Puy.)*

When you reach the top (modern factory building on R) KSO(L) at fork down wide gravelled lane alongside high stone wall, passing below octagonal building on LH side. Lane then > an unsurfaced road. *Good views all round.* At the crossing of five tracks KSO, passing stone wayside cross (to your L, with notice telling you there are 1695km to Santiago, though these, and subsequent indications of this sort, are not necessarily accurate). KSO, climbing gradually, and ignoring turnings to L and R for 2.5k m until you reach the D589.

5.5km La Roche 872m (5.5/732.5)
Junction with GR3, which coincides, going SW, with the GR65 for a short distance.

Either turn L along D589 for 800m or, as the *balises* indicate (and to avoid walking on the road), cross over and KSO on walled lane for 800m then turn L for 400m back to road (making a triangular detour). Then either turn L (from road) or cross road (from track) onto a very minor tarred road and then turn hard R onto upper of two paths. KSO, ignoring turnings and then descend slightly (lane > FP) to join another tarred lane below you and follow this round to the R behind houses.

About 50m before you reach the road again turn L down grassy track, slightly downhill, which then > a FP. KSO, avoiding turns and maintaining your height, as the path winds its way along the shoulder of the hillside, // to the river *Gazelle* in the valley bottom below you to the L. *(TV mast on skyline ahead.)* Path follows low wall on your R for a while *(be careful in foggy weather as although it is fairly wide there is a steep drop to your L – you are walking along a ridge)*. Path then goes on to open grassland. When you come to a T-junction with a farm track (1km later, coming from the R) KSO(L), descending slightly to small wayside cross on L.

There are a lot of wayside crosses in this area marking the pilgrim routes, but although they may seem like the equivalent of our modern waymarks, in centuries gone by they were often used to mark the site of a local shrine or pilgrimage. KSO(R) here at fork *(this is where the GR65 and the GR3 separate)*, taking the uphill/level track to the R (the GR3 goes L *down*hill here) and KSO along grassy track that > a shady walled lane before it begins to descend slowly to cross small humpbacked bridge over stream. KSO again, along tree-lined lane rising gently until you reach the **Place de l'Eglise** in the village of…

3km Saint-Christophe-sur-Dolaison 908m (8.5/729.5)

Bar/tabac (doesn't do food but you can eat your own if you buy a drink), L'Auberge du Grand Chemin (X Mon, does meals T–F midday and Sat evening), boulangerie + limited groceries, ♣ by Mairie. 12th-century church built of pink basalt rock, with interesting bell-tower and statue of St Roch pilgrim inside, château/*seigneurie*.

Pass to LH side of church *(Mairie, phone box, ♣ and PTT all on your L on road)*, turn L (**Rue du Château**) and then turn R along the D31, passing remains of communal bread oven on RH side. About 100m later on turn R (**Place du Lavoir**, *seats, picnic tables)* at small junction down minor road marked 'Tallode 0,5km', skirt the *seigneurie*'s perimeter wall, go under main road (D906) and KSO(L) by wayside cross on other side. Continue through hamlets of **Tallode** *(0.5km, CH, gîte de groupe X Dec/Jan, 14pl, 04.71.03.17.78 & 06.18.11.38.06)* and **Liac** *(0.7km further)*, turning L at end after wayside cross on R by house on L then R down walled lane (track ahead of you continues as grassy track) marked 'Lic 1km'. Continue to hamlet of **Lic** (1km, lane enters open plateau land) and at end, as lane turns L, turn R at side of building up stony track which then opens out to grassy field and KSO alongside low wall on your L, later with low walls on *both* sides. After 400m turn 2nd L down similar lane at right-angle junction and cross very minor tarred road

200m later. *(Variante via **Bains** – three CH, 2 bakeries, 2 restaurants, Church of Sainte-Foy de Conques – begins here).* KSO on other side. *(Montbonnet visible on hillside ahead.)* At staggered junction of five similar tracks turn L (not hard L – *TV mast now ahead on skyline*) and 200m later fork R. KSO along this lane until you reach the D621 and turn R along it at the entrance to the village of…

5.5km Ramourouscle 1030m (14/724)

♣ by junction, 17th-century wayside cross (with seat) and, on L, the first of several *métiers à ferrer les boeufs* that you will see along the way – a device for holding oxen in place while they were fitted with shoes.

In centre of village turn L onto smaller road marked 'Montbonnet 2'. KSO for 1.5km, ignoring turns, until you reach the…

1.5km Chapelle Saint-Roch (15.5/722.5)

Early 13th-century Romanesque chapel, the first of many along the way dedicated to the patron saint of pilgrims. It was originally dedicated to St James, then St Bonnet (a local saint) and then, in the 17th century, to St Roch. Inside there are two engravings of St Roch as a pilgrim and one statue. Chapel is normally open though it was closed for repairs in July 2009 when this guide was being updated.

Continue on road for 500m, passing the **Croix des Pélerins** to the village of…

0.5km Montbonnet 1108m (16/722)

2 gîtes d'étape: a) Gîte d'étape privé l'Escole (04.71.57.51.03, 1/3–4/10, 15 pl); b) Gîte d'étape La Grange/Bar Bar Saint-Jacques (04.71.57.54.44, open all year, 7/7 May–Oct). CH La Barbelotte (06.74.45.51.13) on main road to L on entry, run by two ex-pilgrims, open all year. Café-restaurant Le Grand Duc on entry to village, 7/7 April–Sept, otherwise tel. 04.71.57.53.02.

Continue on road, following it through village, uphill, to junction with D589. (Turn R for gîte.) Turn L on road and 150m later turn R up gravelled lane just before the bar. *(From here to the **Lac d'Oeuf** the GR65 and GR40 coincide.)* About 1km later turn R at junction, uphill towards woods. Fork L at next fork, turn L at next junction and then, when track levels out, follow path to a T-junction.

Pilgrim path between Liac and Lic

When you reach a tarred forest road turn L along it. After 100m fork R down grassy track, descending gradually all the time. Reach a road, cross it and turn R down a second road (behind D589) leading into hamlet of...

4.5km Le Chier 1050m (20.5/717.5)
♣ by Mairie, 2 CH: a) 04.71.57.29.37 & 06.60.38.25.34 b) 04.71.57.20.46.

KSO(L) in centre at tall wayside cross (where road bends round to R) down tarred lane alongside a *couderc* (a sort of village green). Lane > walled, continuing to descend, with fields on either side. Fork R 200m later down wide FP, descending steadily all the time. Pass turning (back L) marked 'Croix du Grand Rocher' and KSO. Around 200m later, when track starts to go uphill, turn L down wide FP, which > a narrow walled lane then a forest path, winding its way steeply down to the valley bottom where it crosses a wooden bridge by an old mill over the **Ruisseau du Rouchoux**. (NB This section could be very slippery in wet weather.) Continue on other side, passing in front of houses. Tarred lane climbs gently and joins D589 coming from back R. Turn L along it into village of...

49

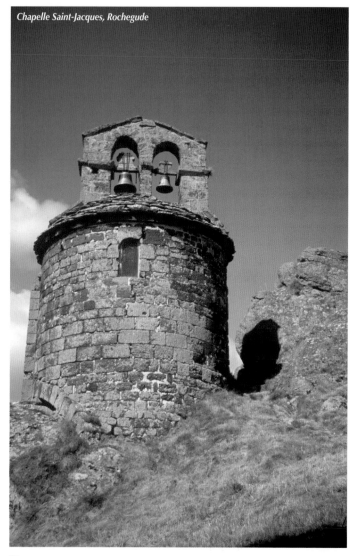

Chapelle Saint-Jacques, Rochegude

3km Saint-Privat-d'Allier 890m (23.5/714.5)

Shops, hotel, Gîte d'Etape La Cabourne at end of village (04.71.57.25.50, open 15/3–15/10, 47 pl K), Accueil bénévolé des pèlerins at first house on R on main road at entry to village (04.71.57 21.56 but no reservations, X 1/10–15/10, donation, K), Gîte-Bar le Kompost'L (04.71.57.24.78, all year, 7/7 but X Mon Oct–May), municipal campsite 04.71.57.22.13, May–Oct), another bar (X Thurs), 2 shops (7/7 but X Mon out of season), TO, ♣ . Romanesque church, remains of château.

To continue, KSO(R) ahead at junction in centre of village between café and bakery, pass Mairie (R) then turn L at next junction onto another minor road, veering L then, at bend (*3 very large crosses and picnic table to R*), fork L onto FP along side of hill with wall to LH side. Reach D301 by iron cross, turn R then L 100m later, after town place-name board and large electric pylon, onto small FP downhill which > a small walled lane. Cross stream and go uphill again to road (short-cutting bend on road). (*In winter, however, or in very wet weather, you might consider staying on the road until the path crosses it again as the FP may be flooded, like walking down a stream.*) Reach small FB, cross stream and KSO uphill to road again. Cross over and continue on other side up to a minor road.

Turn R here, then L almost immediately at a crossing opposite a large house, up wide cobbled walled lane. About 200m later turn L onto tarmac lane past small groups of buildings (this is **Combriaux**); 200m after that KSO at fork, and then 100m later, by bend in road, fork R up FP uphill. Reach minor road again shortly afterwards, turn R along it for 500m then, by sharp RH bend, fork R up FP into the woods, // to road below. Return to road 200m later and look out for FP to L (*view of tower in Rochegude suddenly comes into view ahead*) and fork L down it through woods. About 400m later emerge at crossing at entrance to…

3km Rochegude 967m (26.5/711.5)

Tower, tiny chapel dedicated to St James perched on top of rocky belvedere, the only surviving remains, apart from the tower, of a 13th-century castle complex. Wooden statue of St James pilgrim inside. Commanding views on a clear day. (Beware of straying too far away from chapel if foggy as there are very steep drops on two of its sides.)

To see chapel and tower go up grassy track ahead. To continue turn L downhill.

Go down rocky FP which descends steadily and steeply (the descent from here down to Monistrol can be very slippery in wet weather). KSO(L) at fork. When you reach a road (at entrance to hamlet of **Pratclaux**, ♣, where you can, in fact, continue on road for 1.4km directly to Monistrol) turn L for 50m then fork L (opposite a RH turn down a 'no entry' road) off road up short walled lane. At top turn L and immediately R onto tarred lane through hamlet. After last house on R, turn R down grassy walled lane, veering L, cross road at bottom and KSO down another walled lane on other side. Turn R onto road at end and 100m later turn L down unsurfaced track. At T-junction turn R down grassy lane which > a FP, winding its way steeply down to road (again cutting out zigzags). Turn L and KSO on road then turn R downhill. KSO. Pass turning to a small FP to L, indicating a direct route to the municipal gîte d'étape. If you are not taking this, KSO downhill into **Rue des Poseurs** (named after those who worked laying the railway line, open 1870), veering R and leading to the D589. Pass Mairie and veer L to cross box bridge (built by Gustave Eiffel, of tower fame, in 1888) over the river **Allier** into...

4km Monistrol-d'Allier 619m (30.4/707.5)

SNCF (Paris–Clermont-Ferrand–Arvant–Nîmes), Hotel-Restaurant, CH. Gîte d'étape at Centre d'Accueil, 1.5km before village on Le Puy road (04.71.57.24.14 & 04.71.57.21.21. eve, 12pl, open March–October, K). Gîte d'étape & table d'hôte 'La Tsabone' (04.71.06.17.23 & 06.72.57.62.43, 10-12pl, K, all year). Municipal campsite by river (1/4–15/9). Café, shop, post office. Romanesque church, former priory of La Chaise-Dieu: cross has carving of pilgrim. You are now in the region of the Margeride. *Note: from Monistrol-d'Allier (619m) to the road by the Domaine de Sauvage (1292m) it is 31km of almost continuous uphill and from Monistrol to the separation with the GR412 after Montaure (6.5km) there is an ascent of 450m (nearly 1500ft): remember this when planning your next day's walk.*

Turn R on other side then L up **Rue des Lombards** (turn L here to visit church, then retrace your steps), veering R. Turn L at end then fork R down road at side of mill (signposted to 'La Madeleine, La Vallete'). Cross bridge over the river **Ance** and then KSO, climbing very steeply. (*Views over Allier gorge and beyond.*) The road zigzags its way uphill, passing first a stone wayside cross and then a metal one. At metal cross turn hard L up stony track to the **Chapelle de la Madeleine** (20m), *thought to have been a grotto originally but faced with stone and made into a chapel in the 17th century.*

Looking back over Monistrol d'Allier

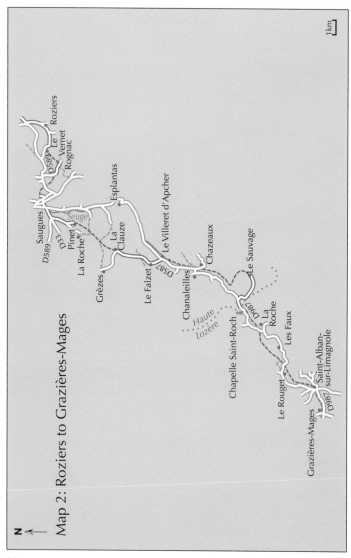

Map 2: Roziers to Grazières-Mages

Then continue very steeply up for another 200m to hamlet of **Escluzels**, turn R and then veer R after first house, pass *lavoir* (L) and another *métier à ferrer les boeufs* to R, with four pillars with remains of leather body and head straps. Turn L uphill on road and KSO. Around 800m later road forks: KSO(L) uphill again, but after 150m turn hard L up wide forest path, short-cutting hairpins in road. Cross road at top, go up narrow path and cross road again and fork L uphill off road on other side up another forest track. Continue uphill, zigzagging steeply, to…

4km Montaure 1022m (34.5/703.5)
View over to Rochegude on opposite side of valley.

When you reach a road KSO(L) ahead *(iron cross on R, ♣)*, veer L again at junction shortly afterwards (modern concrete wayside cross on R: this is the junction with the GR412). Continue on road (L) for 300m, then turn L onto track. KSO, ignoring turns, climbing gently all the time. *(Good views all round.)* When you reach the hamlet of **Roziers** *(1.9km, 1066m, ♣ by lavoir on entry)* KSO(R) on road through village. At a road junction after 0.6km turn R downhill *(the GR412 goes on ahead, to Pouzas)* to the village of…

3.5km Le Vernet de Saugues 1050m (38/700)
Fountain

Continue through village, turn L *(uphill)* at *fountain* and KSO(L). Around 30–40km later turn R by iron cross perched on top of large rock. KSO(L) along gravel track straight ahead, to LH side of woods. About 800m later track > FP through fields. KSO and reach road coming from back L at approach to hamlet of **Rognac**. KSO ahead, pass iron cross (L) and continue ahead uphill. About 700m later when road bends round to R by some houses KSO(L) down green lane towards HT pylon. Continue down it, descending gradually all the time until you reach the D589. *(Note the unusual wooden*

Detail of tree sculpture with St James, entering Saugues

sculptures to LH side of road, made from single trees. You will also see several others in this area.) Cross the road and descend, on the **Rue des Cimes**, into…

4.5km Saugues 960m (42.5/695.5)

Population 2000. 2 hotels, bars, restaurants, shops, banks (+ATM), post office, TO in Cours Gervais, CH. Gîte d'étape communal, Rue de la Margeride (in centre of village, 04.71.77.80.62 & 06.65.15.04.32, 17pl, all year, K). Accommodation (+ meals if required) at Centre d'Accueil, Rue des Tours Neuves (04.71.77.60.97, 40pl), Mar–Oct). Gîte à la ferme, Rue des Roches (04.71.77.83.45, 15/3–1/10. 2 CH: a) 04.71.77.86.92, b) 04.71.77.67.91 & 06.65.30.40.13). Campsite by river (15/4–15/10).

Romanesque church of Saint-Médard (and treasury), diorama de Sainte-Bénilde (a local saint), 13th-century Tour des Anglais with dungeon, numerous old houses. Saugues was the meeting point of pilgrims coming from the Auvergne via secondary routes and had a 12th-century pilgrim hospital (now an old people's home near the Chapelle des Pénitents) dedicated to St James.

If you have not already come across this phenomenon before you may be surprised to encounter (from the south of France and onwards) the first of many church and other public clocks (on civic buildings, for example) that strike *twice* for every hour (and therefore 24 times at midnight…). Since many of them do not have the 'ding dong ding dong' prelude to the actual hour strokes that are customary on British clocks, the first series is, in effect, an announcement that the hour is going to strike – for the second time – after a couple of minutes' pause.

At entrance to town veer L along **Rue de la Demoiselle**, then turn R along **Route du Puy** (main street) into centre. Turn L into **Rue Saint-Gervais** and continue via **Rue Saint-Médard**, **Place Joseph Limozin**, **Rue de la Margeride** (D589 in direction of *Le Malzieu*) and **Route Mont du Mouchet** *(campsite below R)*. Cross D585 at bottom *(note another very large wooden sculpture with pilgrim motifs)* and then bridge over river **Seuge**. About 150m later turn L down track. At road 700m later turn L uphill, forking L at metal wayside cross 0.6km before hamlet of **Le Pinet** (1020m). KSO on road through hamlet. At last house road > track, veering R, climbing gently towards conifer woods ahead. About 200m later KSO(L) at fork. KSO ignoring turns. After reaching a col the track levels out and then descends gently to cross stone bridge over the **Seuge**. KSO(R) on other side. Track > walled lane, climbing gently all the time. Ignore turns to L and R. At the top of a hill 700m later enter…

7.5km La Clauze 1095m (50/688)

Gîte à la ferme Au Repos d'Antan (04.71.77.66.56 & 06.66.47.67.18, 7pl, 15/4–15/10, K). Freestanding tower is the only surviving remains of the late 12th-century castle.

At junction of five tracks at entrance to hamlet KSO ahead on minor tarred road coming from back R. When you meet another (bigger) road coming from back R, near tower, KSO along it through village and continue on road (D335). At top of hill (five-way junction) fork L ahead downhill on minor tarred road to…

2.5km Le Falzet 1134m (52.5/685.5)

Gîte d'étape (04.71.74.42.28, 7pl, 1/3–1/10, K). Picnic area behind gîte.

Continue through hamlet to road, turn L uphill and 40m later fork R up track leading to…

1.5km Villeret-d'Apcher (54/684)

Gîte d'Etape l'Auberge des Pèlerins run by two former pilgrims (06.07.28.06.44, 19pl, Mar–Oct, K). ♣ .

At entrance to village track > tarred road. Cross D587 (slightly staggered junction) and go down narrow street on other side, opposite gîte d'étape, veering L, and then turn R downhill to cross river **Virlange** and KSO(L) ahead on other side, uphill. Continue uphill and near top, at crossing, turn R, veering L downhill. Reach T-junction with tarred lane ahead and turn L onto sandy track, continuing along side of hill. Reach small tarred road and turn R up to the farm at…

2.5km Contaldès 1143m (56.5/681.5)

Pass to L of farm, KSO(L) ahead up a walled lane, along a line of telegraph poles.

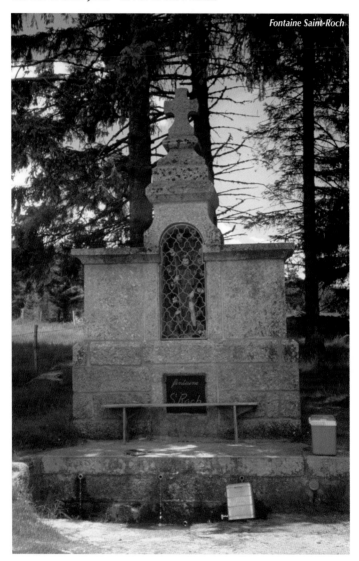

Fontaine Saint-Roch

Village across valley to R, with cemetery, is Chanaleilles (1km, 1170m), with shop (7/7), Café du Pont (does meals, ask here for gîte d'étape, 04.71.74.41.63, 12pl, 15/3–15/11). CH/bar, Place de la Mairie (04.71.74.41.74, all year). Interesting Romanesque church. To go there, fork R on tarred lane in Contaldès, instead of continuing straight ahead.

KSO to **Chazeaux** (800m) and then turn L in centre of village, steeply uphill then turn R, still uphill but then levelling out. Reach junction with minor road then continue on other side on sandy track, undulating. KSO. Turn L at fork, veering R. KSO. Enter woods and KSO. Go through small gate and KSO. About 1.5km later go through 2nd gate and turn L uphill on other side. Some 250m later turn R onto more level track and 300m after that leave woods. Around 250m later turn R through wooden gate onto farm track, widing its way through pastureland. *(The small isolated stone house to R is a* buron, *a shepherd's bothy used during the summer when cattle and flocks of sheep are brought up to graze in the high pasturelands.)* KSO and 600m later reach the…

5.5km Domaine du Sauvage 1292m (62/676)

A historic monument, the former Domerie (hospital run by a religious order) des Templiers, dating from the 13th century. Gîte d'étape, 04.71.74.40.30, 40pl, all year, K, no meals available but food for sale).

Pass farm buildings and then veer round to R by small lake and continue through woods. KSO to road by ski-chalet Saint-Roch and then turn L. KSO for 300m to **Fontaine Saint-Roch** *(site of 13th-century oratory as well as pilgrim hospital from 12th to 17th centuries., after which it fell into ruins)* with picnic site. About 300m later, at border of the *départements* of the *Haute Loire* (that you are leaving) and the *Lozère* (that you are now entering) reach…

3.5km Chapelle Saint-Roch 1280m (65.5/672.5) ♣

Also known as **Chapelle de l'Hospitalet du Sauvage**, this was a hospital for pilgrims and travellers, founded at this col in 1198, and originally dedicated to St James (chapel was next to present fountain). The chapel was rededicated to St Roch after the Wars of Religion (1562–98), but then fell into ruin. The new chapel built at the end of the 19th century was destroyed by a cyclone in 1897, and the present one was rebuilt in 1901. Usually locked,

▶

but a grille in the door enables you to see inside. Statue of St Roch with his dog above the altar. Sunday Mass 11:15 July to Sept and an annual local pilgrimage on 16th August, the feast day of St Roch. Refuge on road (clean and well kept, fountain at rear) is a useful place to rest, eat or shelter in bad weather.

About 100m later, when road bends R, KSO(L) downhill on wide grassy track. (Waymarks tell you there are now 'only' 1478 km left to Santiago…) *The section from here down to Saint-Alban is easy walking.* Continue through semi-shaded woods. At end cross another track and KSO on walled lane. After 2km cross D987.

KSO on other side, gently downhill all the time. Almost at the valley bottom there is a junction with the GR4 *(you can also turn L here for the two gîtes)*, and the GR65 and GR4 continue for a short stretch in common. Cross the river **Gazamas** at the bottom and KSO uphill into pinewoods. At junction with forest road gîte d'étape at **Les Faux** is signposted to L *(L'Oustal de Parent, 10min away, 04.66.31.50.09, 19pl, March–October, K).* KSO(L) along wide forest road joining from back R *(here the GR65 and GR4 part company again).*

KSO, slightly downhill all the time. When the road veers L, KSO(R) ahead down grassy lane. This leads downhill all the time. At T-junction (and with road below you now) turn R and 700m later reach the D987 again (♣ *at crossing*) in the hamlet of…

6km Le Rouget 1017m (71.5/666.5)

Gîte d'Etape à la Ferme la Croix du Plô, on GR65 500m after leaving village (04.66.31.53.51 & 06.33.55.61.03, 9pl, all year, K).

The village takes its name from the red stone in the area. From here onwards the style of building changes and the red-tile roofs characteristic of the area up to and including Saugues give way to grey slate.

Cross road and veer R down minor road which > track. At bottom (100m later), KSO(L) on minor road coming from back R, pass metal wayside cross and KSO. At bottom of hill (end of hamlet) turn R down track which passes under HT cables. When this bends L at farm building *(gîte d'étape La Croix de Plô is here).* KSO(R) down smaller track which leads to the D987 (coming from back R) at entry to **Saint-Alban-sur-Limagnole**. At junction in front of you veer L down minor road marked 'Hôpital' and with football pitch on L (this is the **Chemin de Compostelle**). Turn R at end, veering L then R round to front of hospital, downhill all the time. Pass in front of château *(turn R up steps, then up more steps for TO inside)*, continue downhill then turn L down flight of steps. After that either go down a second set of steps into the **Grand'Rue** or turn R and then L into it.

3.5km Saint-Alban-sur-Limagnole 950m (75/663)

Small town (population 2000) with 2 hotels (all year), 3 CH (all year), shops, restaurants, bars. Gîte d'Etape privé, 14 Grand'Rue (04.66.31.58.69 & 06.32.24.43.17, 10pl, all year, K). Gîte d'Etape La Penote, 19 Route de Saugues (04.66.31.54.13 & 06.88.24.51.32, 4pl, all year X 1/8–15/8, K.). Accueil bénévole La Maison du Pèlerin, 37 Grand'Rue (04.66.45.74.33, 1/4–30/10, donation). *Gîte d'étape* on top floor of Hôtel du Centre (04.66.31.50.04, 16pl, closed out of season), bank (with ATM), TO (in castle, Rue de l'Hôpital). Campsite at end of town (1/3–1/11), 500m after GR turn-off. Romanesque church of Saint-Alban in town centre (red sandstone and polychrome brick). Château (various dates) is now part of the regional psychiatric hospital.

In **Grand'Rue** turn R in front of church, then L down its side (ie when facing entrance) and L down **Rue de la Tournelle** to the **Hôtel de Ville**. Turn L along road (**Rue de la Baysse**) to D987 and turn R along it for 400m, turning R at end of town up gravelled lane just after sports ground and town exit boards. *(Campsite marked 500m further on on road.)* Go up lane through trees, uphill to tall stone cross at top then downhill, ignoring turns, to road in hamlet of…

2km Grazières-Mages 930m (77/661) ☂

Turn hard L along road, veer R *(at iron cross in front of you)* downhill and then veer L to cross river **Limagnole**. Cross D587 and veer R steeply uphill on gravel path through semi-shaded woods, levelling out onto an open plateau at the top. Reach road in hamlet of **Chabannes** (2km) and veer R along it downhill *(note stocks on RH side)* passing (R) another of the tall stone crosses typical of the Lozère and KSO.

When road veers L at second stone cross (small), KSO(R) down shady lane along line of telegraph poles, then turn 2nd R at staggered junction on track coming from road at back L. Continue on ridge *(good views)*, enter woods and descend, gradually at first and then more steeply, down to road, turning L and then R round church in…

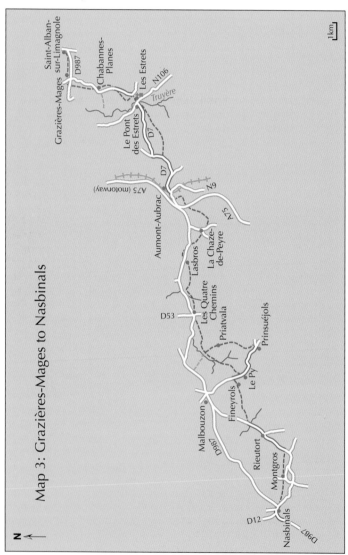

Map 3: Grazières-Mages to Nasbinals

5.5km Les Estrets 940m (82.5/655.5)

Gîte d'étape (04.66.45.61.90 & 06.88.90.97.89, 20pl, 1/4–10/10, also CH), Bar du Pont (X Wed, does food), phone box, fountain. Formerly a commandery of the order of St John of Jerusalem, controlling the passage over the Truyère; hence its name: '*étroits*' = 'straits'. Present church dates from 1866, replacing previous one (though plaque on wall refers to 'chapelles' being rebuilt); statue of St Roch inside, and lectern has carvings of scallop shell, scrip and pilgrim staff.

Turn R along road (D7) *(church to R)* and continue through village *(note small stone cross with figure of Christ on LH side)* veering L *(gîte signposted to R)* to D806. Cross over and veer R to cross old bridge over the **Truyère** in hamlet of **Le Pont des Estrets** (1km).

Turn L up track between two houses and continue steeply uphill. After 1km reach minor road at a bend *(iron cross)* and turn L downhill into hamlet of **Bigosse**. *(New gîte d'étape due to open late 2009, Les Granges de Bigosse.)* Veer round to R and KSO(R) along track, undulating along RH side of valley then veering to LH side before veering L uphill along side of woods, climbing steadily all the time. Enter wood and continue to climb uphill continuously.

Emerge into small clearing at top and KSO(R) along similar track coming from back L by modern wayside cross, slightly downhill. Continue ahead, pass metal wayside cross and then start climbing again until, 1km later, you reach the…

4km Route D7 1096m (86.5/651.5)

Turn R along D7 for 100m then turn hard L on gravel track. Opposite an industrial building fork R down shady walled lane with small stone cross with scallop shell at start, // to road. *(Note the prayer and scallop shell on tree to L.)* After 1km reach road again at iron cross, turn R down minor road (**Route de la Margeride**) for 400m, rejoining road again by junction with iron cross. KSO and at bend continue ahead down some steps into **Rue du Barri Haut** (gîte d'étape on RH side), cross over main road by large iron cross, continue on other side, go down **Rue du Prieuré** and turn L down side of TO to church. Turn L uphill *(note 1708 Mater Dolorosa in niche at first-floor level on L)* and go up to **Place du Portail** (**Hôtel de Ville**) in the centre of town, where there is a statue of the Bête du Gévaudan, *the beast renowned in the area as being responsible for the mysterious disappearance*

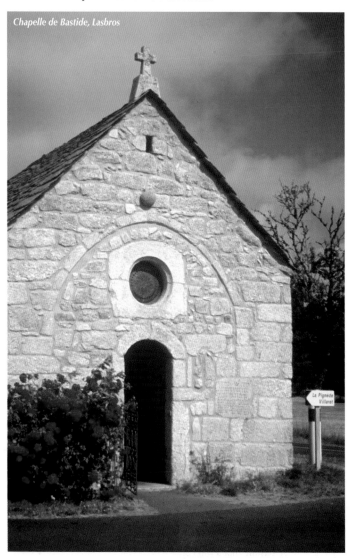

Chapelle de Bastide, Lasbros

of some 50 people between 1765 and 1768; a lynx killed near Saint-Flour in 1787 was thought to have been the culprit.

3km Aumont-Aubrac 1050m (89.5/648.5)

Small town (population 1050) with three hotels; shops, cafés, bank (ATM by post office), TO Rue de l'Eglise. a) Gîte d'étape & CH La Ferme du Barry at entrance to the town, 9 Rue du Barry (04.66.42.90.25 & 06.71.83.17.46, 24pl, Easter to 1/11). b) Gîte d'Etape Les Sentiers Fleuris, 7 Place du Portail (04.66.42.94.70 & 06.42.64.80.02, 20pl, 15/3–31/10), also CH. c) Bar-gîte d'Etape Le Calypso in Aubrac Hôtel, Place du Forail (04.66.42.99.00). d) Accueil Chrétien, Salle Paroissiale Saint-Etienne (04.66.32.80.92, mass daily 18:00, Sat 20:30 July/Aug, Sun 11:00. Open 14:30–18:30 July/Aug, spartan, no beds, shower, K). Municipal campsite, Route du Languedoc (June–Sept). SNCF (train service now replaced by buses) to Clermont-Ferrand.

Former Benedictine Priory and Romanesque church of Saint-Etienne; restored in 1994, it now has splendid modern stained-glass windows.

Continue ahead on main road (that is to your R, **Avenue du Peyre**) and then fork R at war memorial on **route d'Aubrac**. Go under railway line and turn L along minor road alongside it. About 200m later fork R up fenced lane leading to side of woods *(iron cross to L)* and KSO uphill, passing under HT cables. Turn R at top along road for 300m and then fork L to track (just after town name board). After 150m turn L and then R to go under motorway via a specially placed 'pilgrim tunnel' *(referred to locally as the 'Saintjacqueduc')*. Turn R on other side and then L to continue on a level track leading to woods. Continue along it, descending gradually to the **Route de la Chaze** (3.5km, *stone cross*, 1016m). Turn R along it for 1km (tip of church spire visible), KSO(R) at fork by cemetery and enter village of…

4.5km La Chaze-du-Peyre 1040m (94/644)

Phone box, ♣. Two crosses in square in front of church, one 18th-century, the other 19th. Church of varying periods including St James's chapel.

Continue through village on road, passing church and veering R uphill, forking L between drinking trough and iron cross onto minor road signed 'Lasbros'. After 1km, at junction with D987 *(the old Roman road from Lyon to Toulouse – the Voie d'Agrippa – that would have been used by pilgrims in centuries gone by)* reach the tiny **Chapelle de Bastide** *(not always open), begun in 1522 but reworked several* *times and sometimes referred to as 'La Chapelette'. (Shortly afterwards there is a wooden bus shelter, useful for a rest in bad weather, with another in the hamlet of Lasbros ahead.)* Continue on D987 into the hamlet of…

2km Lasbros 1091 (96/642)

Gîte (04.66.47.08.94, 6pl, all year, K). Fountain, phone box.

At end of hamlet fork L down minor tarred road. Continue downhill, KSO(R) at fork and continue uphill, road > track. KSO, fork L at T-junction, then turn L along minor road which also > a track. KSO, gently uphill all the time *(and watching out carefully for hunters with shotguns in the open season…)*. Pass first turning (L) to **Prinsuéjols** *(waymarked in red and yellow)* and KSO, veering R at very end to road junction known as…

4km Les Quatre Chemins 1174m (100/638)

Café 'Chez Régine' (picnic with own food possible if purchasing a drink), sandwiches.

Continue ahead on road to join D587 coming from back R then turn L down forest track. KSO 100m later down track fenced in with barbed wire through grassy plateau land, undulating, with occasional shade. *(In bad weather some parts of the track are very boggy.) Like other areas of the Margeride and the Aubrac this is a paradise of wild flowers in the springtime.* Shortly after track > a walled lane. You reach a T-junction with another walled lane to L, opposite cattle pen on R and with grove of trees ahead.

*If you want to sleep in the gîte d'étape in **Prinsuéjols** (1205m, 3.8km due south, bar/restaurant, 04.66.32.52.94, 45pl) you can turn L here and follow the red-and-yellow balises of the GR du Pays known as the 'Tour des Monts d'Aubrac'. If so, you do not need to retrace your steps the following morning but can take the D73 northwards from Prinsuéjols in the direction of Malbouzou, passing through the hamlet of **Pratviala**; this road crosses the GR65 further to the west, just after the Ferme des Gentianes.* Otherwise, KSO. Go through four *cledos*, cross road leading to L to **Pratviala** and KSO. Track > unsurfaced road (more *cledos*). When you reach a bend in the road *(iron cross ahead, the Croix de Ferluc)* continue to road (farm to R) and KSO on minor tarred road. About 100m later reach cross-roads with the D73 at the…

Communal oven, Rieutort d'Aubrac

5km Ferme des Gentianes 1192m (105/633)

Farm (04.66.32.52.77) does meals, has gîte d'étape (19pl, 15/3–31/10, K, camping possible) and CH.

KSO ahead, go through hamlet of **Fineyrols** (♣ *and picnic area to L*) and fork R uphill at end (> track), wending its way through grassy plateau land strewn with big boulders. KSO, ignoring turns. Track > grassy walled lane, climbing gradually across the deserted Aubrac plateau. *(Splendid views on a clear day.)* At the top of the plateau (1273m, **Roc des Loups**) KSO alongside wall on L, descending gradually. This is the **Grande Draille**, *a historic drove road*, veering R (to become walled lane again) and then L. At T-junction with gravelled lane turn R, and 200m later turn L along minor road at the **Pont sur la Peyrade** and KSO to...

4.5km Rieutort d'Aubrac 1158m (109.5/628.5)

♣ , phone box. (CH 2km to L at Marchastel, on GR65A, 04.66.32.53.79, April–Nov) New *gîte d'étape* 'L'Ange Gardien' at entrance to village on R. (Note two granite drinking troughs, communal oven and the remains of another *métier pour ferrer le boeufs*.)

67

A 20km variante *route to Aubrac or directly to Saint Chely d'Aubrac – the GR56A plus GR6 and/or GRP – turns L here via* Marchastel, Lac de Saint-Andéol, *Gallo-Roman site* Ad Silanum *and* Pendouliou-de-Fabrègues, *1359m. It is marked on the green series maps but is not waymarked and is an even more deserted route, only recommended in good weather and for experienced walkers.* Otherwise, continue on through village, veering R and KSO (1.8km) to junction with D900 at the **Pont de Marchastel** over the river **Bès**. Turn R over bridge and 60m later turn R up track. When you reach a road veer R up it into village of...

3.5km Montgros 1234m (113/625)

Private gîte d'étape/hotel La Maison de Rosalie (04.66.32.55.14, all year X 15 days in March and November, auberge (meals, rooms, café), 2nd bar/auberge but variable opening hours.

Continue on road to end of village and at crossroads *(iron cross)* KSO ahead down track undulating between fields. Cross minor road and KSO uphill ahead. At crossing continue downhill to road *(stone cross)*. Turn R along D900 to...

3km Nasbinals 1180m (116/622)

Four hotels, municipal gîte (Maison Richard, Rue Principale, 04.66.32.59.47 & 04.66.32.50.17, 19pl, 1/4–31/10, K), Gîte d'étape privé La Grappière (next to pharmacy, 04.66.32.15.60, 15pl, 15/3–15/10, K). Gîte d'étape in Centre d'Accueil (04.66.32.50.42, 38pl, all year). Gîte de Caractère Lô (04.66.32.92.69 & 06.80.28.51.12, 20pl, all year, K). Gîte-Centre équestre des Monts d'Aubrac (on D12 500m towards Chaudes-Aigues, 04.66.32.50.65, 20pl, all year, RE). Camping municipal, Route de Saint Urcize (1/5–30/9). TO (7/7 in season, X Sun pm Oct –June), pharmacy, bank, boulangerie, épicerie, bars. 11th-century Romanesque church in local stone and style (statue of St Roch inside, together with wooden statues of various other saints): monument with a pair of crutches on its base is to Pierre Brioude ('Pierrounet'), a 19th-century bonesetter and manipulator of joints who is said to have treated over 10,000 people a year.

Cross D987, KSO down small street, veer R and then L around side of church (on D987) and follow road round uphill (municipal *gite d'étape* on R) out of town in the direction of Aubrac. At the end (at **Le Coustat**) turn first R uphill onto tarred

Map 4: Nasbinals to St-Pierre-de-Bessuéjouls

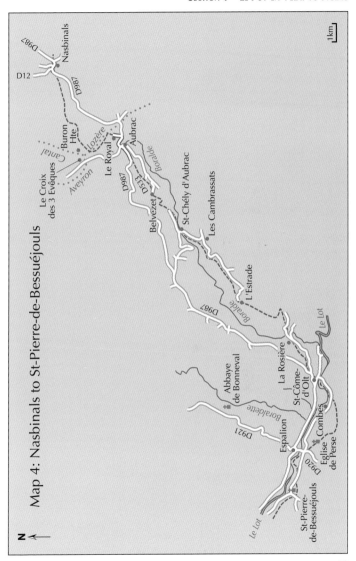

N ←

1km

Nasbinals
D987
D12
D987
Buron Hte
Le Croix des 3 Evêques
Canal
Aveyron
Lozère
Le Royal
Aubrac
Boralde
D987
D533
Belvezet
St-Chély d'Aubrac
Les Cambrassats
L'Estrade
D987
Boralde
Le Lot
La Rosière
Abbaye de Bonneval
Boraldette
St-Côme-d'Olt
D921
Espalion
Combes
Eglise de Perse
D920
Le Lot
St-Pierre-de-Bessuéjouls

69

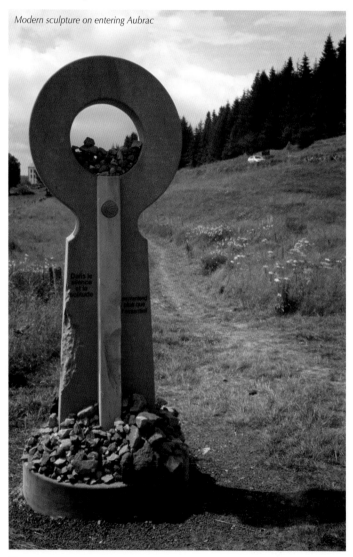

Modern sculpture on entering Aubrac

road which > stony track through woods. Veer L uphill (> walled lane). KSO(R) when you meet another track coming from back L, across undulating plateau land in direction of woods ahead.

About 1km later (at fork marked 'Nasbinals 3km, village 4km') fork L along wooded walled lane. At next fork turn R, cross bridge (**Pont de Pascalet**) over the river **Chambouliès** and continue uphill. Around 100m before farm building ahead turn R over stile, go uphill up side of field alongside wall (to your L), and 100m later turn L through gateway and continue alongside wall. Go over second stile and continue ahead uphill (away from wood to L), following line of tall wooden marker posts, to the…

6km Buron de Ginestouse Bas 1303m (122/616)

Another *buron* (bothy) used during the summer months when shepherds and their flocks were up on the plateau, returning to the valleys in the autumn.

Two small stone houses to R. Go over another stile and KSO ahead, in direction of small group of woods ahead and three small buildings away up the hill to your R ahead *(Ginestouse Haut)*. When you reach a wall go through fourth stile and KSO alongside wall (on your L). *(NB All these stiles have* cledos *next to them but while they are easy enough to open they are often very tricky to shut!)* When the wall veers L at woods follow it round and then KSO above (and // to) woods to your L. Then veer R slightly uphill to follow another wall (again on your L) uphill. Follow wall round to your L, pass between two wooden gate posts.

The blunt, cone-shaped hill above R is the **Trois Evêques***, the border of three bishoprics in the old days, and today the borders of the* départements *of the Cantal, the* Lozère *and the Aveyron, as well as of the old regions of the* Auvergne*, the* Aubrac *and the Midi-Pyrenees. From here you leave the* Lozère *and until just past Conques you are in the* Aveyron*.*

Go through cattle pen (gates at both ends) and KSO alongside wall to your L. Go downhill slightly, through a *cledo* and then KSO ahead uphill (shelter – *abri* – at top) up a very wide walled lane, the **Grande Draille** again. Continue ahead on this, descending to the road *('Village de vacances Royal-Aubrac', a former sanatorium, to R, 05.65.44.28.41, open all year, also has* gîte *d'étape)*. Cross road and continue on path on other side. Modern sculpture, erected 2006, has text *'dans le silence et la solitude'* on its LH side and, on R, *'on n'entend plus que l'éternité'*. At crossing 300m later turn R uphill for church, tower (with gîte d'étape communal inside) and village of…

3km Aubrac 1307m (125/613)

Hôtel-restaurant de la Domerie (05.65.44.28.42, X 15/11–9/2, 2 other restaurants (summer only), café (4/4–11/11). No shops. TO. Gîte d'étape communal in La Tour des Anglais (05.65.44.21.15, 24pl, open mid-May–mid-Sept only, K). CH with 14 pl dormitory (05.65.48.78.84, X 15/11–15/12).

The village of **Domerie d'Aubrac** was founded in 1120 by a Flemish knight, Adelard de Flandres, who was attacked by bandits on his way to Santiago and who almost died there in a storm on his return journey. In gratitude for his deliverance he founded Aubrac as a place of refuge for pilgrims. Church of Notre-Dame des Pauvres has a large panel painting in two parts on the inside wall (1993–94), depicting the history of the Domerie d'Aubrac, from its founding to the late 20th century. The church, plus two other buildings now privately owned, is all that remains of the monastery. Tour des Anglais, botanical garden.

From here you have the option of a 25km waymarked route direct to Espalion via the Cistercian **Abbaye de Bonneval** (simple gîte d'étape, during July and August, 6pl, in its Tour Saint-Jacques). Otherwise, from here to Saint-Chely-d'Aubrac you descend steeply, dropping 500m in 8km (1500ft in only 5 miles). The scenery changes after this, the vast open plateau giving way to gorges and more woods before entering the Lot valley in Saint Côme d'Olt.

Leave Aubrac along the D987 (west). After 800m fork L off road down grassy track. KSO, descending steadily all the time, KSO twice when track joins from back R.

The yellow-flowered plant, approximately 1m high and seen growing every-where around here, is gentiane, whose root is used to make Suze (a liqueur). After large wooden cross fork L on grassy track then at junction fork L downhill, becoming a walled lane *(view of hamlet of Belvezet below and remains of castle perched on top of pillar-like rock).* When you reach two extremely large rocks on hill immediately in front of you fork R down FP, veering L and then R to road in hamlet of...

4km Belvezet 1144m (129/609)

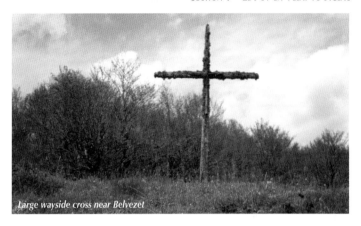
Large wayside cross near Belvezet

Turn L along road and then hard R down lane 100m later. Then turn R and veer R down narrow walled lane downhill. Reach crossing of similar tracks and KSO. About 1km from Belvezet cross the **Aude** and continue L on other side, descending steadily all the time. About 1.5km later pass farm on L (**La Vayssière**) and track > a tarmac lane. *(If you want to go to the Gîte Saint-André or the campsite in Saint-Chély look out for FP on L leading downhill straight there.)* Reach road 200m later at a U-bend in it. Turn L, and KSO down it to junction with main street in **Saint-Chély** and turn R along it. To continue turn L by post office. To go to municipal gîte (further along street on L) KSO.

4km Saint-Chély-d'Aubrac 808m (133/605)

Small town with two hotels, restaurants, shop, bar, TO Rue de la Tour, post office (+ ATM), ☗. Gîte d'étape communal, Route d'Espalion (05.65.44.21.15, 26pl, 1/5–31/10, K). Gîte d'Etape Saint-André (on L at entry to village, 05.65.44.26.87, 20pl, all year, K). Bar Le Relais Saint-Jacques & CH (05.65.44.12.96 & 05.65.48.78 or 89). CH La Tour des Chapelains (next to TO, 05.65.51.64.80 & 06.69.14.33.38). Camping municipal (15/5–31/8). 15th-century church has gold statue of St Roch pilgrim to LH side of wall behind altar (with a lot of scallop shells on his lapel, stick, hat, dog and gourd), a stained glass window of St Roch pilgrim to the L of the apse and an unusual statue of St Peter with a cockerel at his feet.

From Saint-Chély-d'Aubrac to Figeac the GR65 and GR6 share the same route. Turn L by post office (**Rue de la Mairie**), veering R into **Place Joseph-Bond** (in front of the Mairie), turn L down side of the **Ecole Publique** into the **Rue du Pont des Pèlerins** (turn L here into **Rue de l'Eglise** to visit church then retrace your steps) and KSO down narrow street winding its way down to cross the old bridge over the **Boralde**. *(Note 16th-century cross on bridge with tiny pilgrim sculpted in its base, with his stick and rosary.)* Veer L, R and then L on other side to cemetery and then turn hard R at 'stop' sign onto a track leading uphill behind cemetery, which then > a walled lane, climbing steeply to the road (D19). Turn R uphill and 300m later (at L bend) KSO(R) downhill on minor road (signed 'Les Combrassats 2') through hamlet of **Le Recours**. About 200m later fork R off road down walled lane, which then > clear forest track, undulating through woods for 2km. KSO, then track climbs uphill again, > FP and rejoins road again. *(Note cross just below road.)*

Turn R along road (just before hamlet of **Combrassats**, 919m). KSO(R) at fork at entry to hamlet, then turn L behind first building on L down a walled lane, undulating, until you reach a disused farm at **Foyt**. Turn L up grassy lane to minor road and then turn R. KSO on ridge *(good views)*, ignoring turns to L and R, descending gradually. After 1.5km pass RH turning to **Bessières** and 150m later fork R off road by small wooden wayside cross onto grassy lane which continues along a ridge. KSO, veering L at end, to hamlet of…

5.5km L'Estrade (138.5/599.5)

♠ , shelter on R (with tables) in former communal oven.

Turn R along road *(handy seat)* which > unsurfaced track along ridge, descending gradually before veering L downhill through woods and later > walled lane between fields. About 4km later veer L at fork and then immediately, at junction with forest road, R (a staggered junction) down through woods again, descending fairly steeply until you cross **Le Cancels** *(stream)* via FB. Go uphill for 100m on other side and turn R on D557 (by 'stop' sign). About 100m later at U-bend in another road KSO ahead on other side by modern wayside cross between the two, down shaded track, forking R shortly afterwards down FP leading to road. Turn L, cross bridge and KSO on road. Just after a bend and before a bridge you will see a sign pointing you steeply uphill on a sandy track. Here you can:

a) KSO ahead on road (D557, little traffic) for 3.5km to Saint Côme d'Olt, via the hamlets of **Martillergues** and **La Rigaldie**, an option suggested in bad weather, joining the high-level route when the **Rue de la Draille** joins the **Route de Castelnau**;

b) turn R uphill (very steep, signed 'La Rozière, Saint Côme'). *This option is a 'scenic detour', 2km longer and only worth it (on account of the views) in very clear, bright weather.* Go uphill, veering L, very steeply to **La Rozière** (fountain) at top. Turn L, go through hamlet and KSO(L) at end down walled lane. Around 300–400m later fork R down narrow walled lane, widening out. Follow it downhill, then up again, and after 500m at farm (**Grèzes**) continue on tarred lane. About 100m later turn L, then 50m after that turn L again onto sandy lane, until you reach the hamlet of **Cinqpeyres**. KSO(L) downhill at fork and continue towards road (*view of church spire ahead*), but just before

Twisted church spire, Saint-Côme d'Olt

you reach road fork L to LH side of house down walled lane. Reach minor road and turn R along it, then L 200m later down **Rue de la Draille**.

At bottom turn R (**Route de Castelnau**) – *twisted spire of the church in Saint-Côme visible ahead from here* – and 20m later cross D987. (*Turn R here if you want to sleep in the Couvent du Malet.*) KSO down lane on other side, veer L near end, turn R along minor road and then L through tunnel under road. KSO up **Rue Mathat** to **Place de la Porte Neuve** in...

10.5km Saint-Côme d'Olt 385m (149/589)

Hotel, shops, 2 restaurants, post office, bank + ATM (Avenue d'Aubrac). Gîte d'étape communal del Romiou in Tour de Greffe (former prison, 05.65.44.07.09, 19pl, 1/4–31/10, K). Espace Angèle Mérici, Couvent de Malet, 500m before town on D987, phone ahead (05.65.51.03.20, donation, rooms with 2–3 beds, all year, Rue de Boraldette (05.65.44.12.58, March to 1/11, K). CH & 5pl gîte Le Jardin d'Eline, 3 Avenue d'Aubrac (05.65.48.28.06 & 06.82.64.04.49, 15/3–31/10). Camping Bellerive, Rue du Terral, near bridge (15/4–30/9, also rents caravans per night), TO.　　▶

Olt is the old name for the river Lot. Medieval town with very few modern buildings. 16th-century church of SS Côme and Damien has twisted spire (similar to the one in Chesterfield), 10th-century Chapelle des Pénitents, formerly with pilgrim hospital dedicated to St James adjoining, Ouradou (pilgrim oratory). 15th and 16th-century houses, 14th-century château is now Hôtel de Ville. Gothic bridge. Historic information on street plaques: walking tour available from TO. Street names are given in both French and Occitan (eg Carrièra la Glèisa = Rue de l'Eglise).

Cross **Place de la Porte Neuve**, go under archway and turn L down **Rue du Greffe** to church. Continue *(church L)* through next arch (**Porte Théron**), turn L, cross **Place de la Barryère** and go down **Rue du Terral**, veering R at iron cross to cross old bridge over the **Lot**. *(Stone cross on bridge.)* Turn R almost immediately down minor road marked 'Combes'.

After 1km along river and after bridge you have a choice between a high-level detour to visit the **Vierge Notre-Dame de Vermus** *(a viewpoint over the whole of the Lot valley with a statue of the virgin on top, worth the climb in splendid weather but not otherwise)*, or continuing along the road to Espalion *(little traffic – though this way you will miss the opportunity to visit the Romanesque Eglise de Perse unless you do a detour)*. If you decide to do this (ie *not* visit the Vierge de Vermus), KSO on road (marked 'Combes') which goes along the river **Lot**. Pass entrance to campsite just outside the town, join the **Rue de Perse** then go through park to riverside walkway, pass gîte d'étape (on R, in **Rue Saint-Joseph**) and reach the **Place du Plô** in the centre of **Espalion**.

Otherwise, to visit the Vierge de Vermus fork L uphill up cobbled walled lane. Go through two gates and continue uphill (**Font-dels-Romieus**, *a fountain used by pilgrims*, to L uphill), veering R onto more level track and KSO. At meadow to R and three ruined buildings start climbing steeply. About 300m below the top turn L onto wide forest track (uphill), passing under telegraph poles. At top turn R along grassy lane along ridge, which then descends gradually, veering R at end onto minor tarred road on hill. Turn R along it, undulating along ridge and passing under two sets of telephone/HT cables. *(Good view over the Lot valley.)*

Ignore RH fork and KSO steeply uphill all the time (track now > unsurfaced road), and at bend to R KSO ahead (marked 'Vierge de Vermus') up FP before descending (ahead) through woods on gravelled lane, turning L down narrow FP 20m later. After passing along LH side of fields re-enter woods and KSO downhill all the time on wider, rocky FP. (To visit Vierge – 15min each way – turn R up steep but clear FP halfway down.) Emerge by house and KSO downhill along gravelled lane. *(View of Espalion ahead and château on hilltop.)* Cross bridge at bottom, behind the…

5km Eglise de Perse 353m (154/584)

Romanesque chapel of Saint-Hilarion (built on site near where he was beheaded by the Saracens in the 8th century) in red stone, former pilgrim halt and priory affiliated to Conques. Very fine carvings on outside, but church is often locked.

To visit church: turn L up side of it and enter via cemetery. To continue: KSO ahead into **Espalion**, via the **Chemin de Perse** then the **Rue de Perse** to the **Place du Plô**.

1km Espalion 342m (155/583)

Busy town (population 4614) with 2 hotels, 5 CH, shops, cafés, 7 restaurants. 2 gîtes d'étape communaux: a) 5 Rue Saint-Joseph, 20pl, K, b) 21 Rue Arthur Canel, 8pl, K, both all year, 06.65.51.10.30 & 06.77.58.53.08 for both. Gîte d'Etape La Halte Saint-Jacques, 8 Rue du Dr. Trémolières, (05.65.66.35.61, 16pl, all year, K). Gîte-type accommodation, K, also available (except July/August) in VVF (*colonie de vacances*), 1.5km outside town on Route de Saint-Pierre, on GR65 (05.65.44.02.15 & 06.30.52.18.57. 1/3–30/11). Centre d'herbergement municipal de Boraldes, Route de Saint-Pierre, (05.65.48.04.08 & 06.07.27.68.67, 65pl, all year). Camping municipal Le Roc de l'Arche, Bou du Forail, 15/3–15/10, also has caravans to rent per night.

Pilgrim bridge over the Lot, built in the reign of St Louis by the Frères Pontiff (a monastic bridge-building order). Renaissance château (1572) and Musée Vaylet, local museum.

From the **Place du Plô** continue ahead R on **Rue Arthur Canel** and reach **Rue Droite**. Cross the end of it (the old bridge is now on your R) and continue along **Quai du Lot**. Cross **Boulevard Joseph Poulenc** (new bridge on R) and continue along river bank (400–500m) until you reach a wayside cross on R. Turn L up **Rue Dr Jean Capoulade** and then R into **Rue Eugène Salette**. KSO to very end of road where it > a lane after last house on L. KSO then turn L 100m later and then R,

Church of Saint-Pierre-de-Bességjouls

before lane goes uphill to become a tarred road leading to junction with D556. Turn R along it (quiet) for 1.5km then turn L up minor road at wayside cross, shortly before hamlet of **Coudoustrimes** ahead. KSO (500m) ignoring turns, to the…

3km Eglise de Saint-Pierre-de-Bessuéjouls 335m (158/580)

One of the oldest churches on the route, 11th-century chapel of Saint-Michel on first floor of bell tower, with 9th-century altar and interesting capitals. Good place for a rest outside, ♣ . CH (05.65.48.20.71, March–November).

KSO on road then turn R over bridge *(fountain to L)*, R again beside Mairie and immediately L uphill, passing to RH side of house and continue up narrow FP which zigzags its way very steeply up hillside through woods. *(In very bad weather, however, when this route will be slippery, you can continue on the road, turn L 500m later and rejoin the GR65 in Verrières via the D556.)* Continue to climb very steeply (FP > wider, rockier/stonier, before becoming a stony track). *(Good view of Espalion to rear.)*

Shortly before the top it levels out and then joins a road at the top. Turn L along it along ridge for 1km to hamlet of **Griffoul**, veer L at end and 200m later turn R off road onto level earth track *(splendid views)* which then undulates before becoming a walled lane along ridge. Later on it descends, gradually at first and then steeply. Turn hard L at T-junction, turn L at fork and 400m later reach gravelled lane by **Château de Beauregard**. Turn R downhill for 100m and turn L along minor road to junction by **Trédou** church *(♣ by cemetery gate)*. Turn L by cemetery* (ie just before church) down minor road into hamlet of **Les Camps**. At end turn R onto tarmac lane between fields. About 300m later, at crossing, KSO ahead on other side on gravel track. Turn L at T-junction then reach minor road and turn R along it, into **Verrières**.

*You can, however, continue ahead to the church, veering R behind it and then L onto the D556, rejoining the GR65 1.5km later at junction by cross** in…

6km Verrières (164/574)

CH (05.65.44.73.76 & 06.89.10.25.90) on GR65

KSO ahead down minor road, veering R, then turn L at junction *(cross**)*. Veer L and then R downhill, forking R *(note building with bell on top to L)* to cross bridge

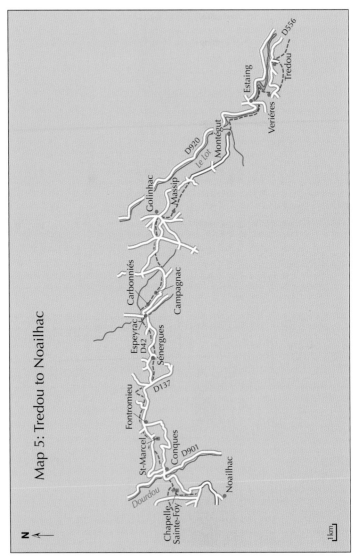

Map 5: Tredou to Noailhac

over stream, with shelter (and seats) opposite.. Turn R and 100m later at junction with D100 turn L down it.

About 500m later, after turning to **La Roque**, either KSO on D100 to Estaing or fork very steeply uphill on stony track, which levels out after a while, becoming FP through woods, more or less // to road below you to R. Descend to the D100 and after 800m reach…

2km Estaing 320m (166/572)

Small town (population 1000) with two hotels, cafés, restaurants, shops, post office +ATM. TO, 24 Rue François d'Estaing. Hospitalité Saint-Jacques, 8 Rue du Collège (small lay community offering lodging to pilgrims, 16pl, donation, no reservations, X families with children under 12, all year, prayers morning and evening). Gîte d'étape communal (05.65.44.71.74 & 05.65.44.70.32, 20pl, 1/3–11/11, K). CH 100m after bridge on GR65 (05.65.44.71.51 & 06.70.38.42.81, all year). Camping municipal La Chantellerie, 15/5–15/9, 2km north of town on D167.

Gothic bridge over the Lot. 15th-century château of the Counts of Estaing is now a convent. 15th-century church of Saint-Fleuret has stone cross outside depicting tiny pilgrim.

Estaing

The GR65 does not go into the town, so to visit: turn R over bridge. To continue, energetic pilgrims have the option of a (4km) shorter route to Conques on the old GR6 via **Saint-Genies des Ers**, **Campuac** *(modern church with fine stained glass)* and **Larrigue**, rejoining the GR65 in **Campagnac**, 3.5km before Espeyrac. To take this option leave Estaing on minor road (marked 'Campuac') to LH side of chapel at end of bridge.

Otherwise, turn L and then immediately R at small chapel on L by bridge (staggered junction), down quiet shady minor road marked 'La Roquette'. This continues for 3km, undulating along the L bank of the **Lot**. At junction (**La Roquette** to R) KSO(L) on same road which then descends to cross bridge over the **Luzanne**. Turn R along road and 100m later turn hard L up very steep narrow FP through woods, the first of several short cuts in the road's mainy hairpins. Turn L at top on road again uphill and 20m later, after hairpin, turn hard L up another FP, zigzagging up to road at a cluster of houses in…

5km Montégut 400m (171/567) ♣

Turn R for 20m then L up another narrow FP, which > forest track, to road at **Montégut Haut**. Turn L on road and continue uphill, climbing steadily. Pass turning to **Rion del Prat** (hard R) and then fork R to **Campredon**. At junction with road from back L just before hamlet of **La Sensaguerie** (530m, *pump to LH side of road*) road begins to level out *(splendid views if clear)*. Continue on road, undulating, mainly shady, then slightly downhill, ignoring turnings. Pass *lieu-dit* **Le Mas**. KSO(L) ahead at R turn to **Castilhac** and shortly before reaching hamlet of **Falguières** fork L uphill off road up grassy track to woods, which > forest track. Climb gradually on and through edge of woods. Cross minor tarred road and KSO ahead down grassy lane, entering woods again, undulating mainly, otherwise climbing steadily.

When you reach a junction at exit from woods (3km after leaving road) turn L uphill. This > a forest road leading, after 1km, to road in hamlet of **Massip** *with gîte d'étape L'Orée du Chemin (05.65.48.61.10 & 06.71.38.07.57, 20pl, all year, K)*. KSO on road for 200m then turn L into woods, just before bend. Reach road again, cross over and continue very steeply downhill on FP through woods to another road below. Turn L and shortly afterwards KSO(R) along lane through woods when road bends L. At T-junction with wayside cross 1km later turn L uphill and then KSO(R) along road to hamlet of **Le Radal** *(gîte équestre, ♣)* and KSO for 300m to road and turn R along it in…

11km Golinhac 650m (182/556)

Shop, bar/restaurant with CH (05.65.51.63.68, all year) and Le Hameau de Saint-Jacques, with 3 gîtes d'étape, (05.65.44.50.73, 43pl, all year, K), Camping Bellevue (May–Sept) and bar-snack are all on L at entry to village. Church of St Martin (statue of St Roch with *coquilles* inside) on site of foundations of 9th-century Benedictine abbey (note cross at entry to village with tiny pilgrim and staff on base).

To continue, pass shop (*gîte and campsite behind it*) and KSO on road to church, turn L and then hard L behind war memorial and immediately R up very minor road, forking L behind houses. Go up walled lane by last house then up tarred lane then at minor road turn R. At crossing KSO down grassy walled lane, veering L to road junction of D42 and D904 in hamlet of **Le Poteau**. KSO ahead along D42 (marked 'Espeyrac 9'). Around 400m later fork R onto grassy lane leading into the woods and uphill on forest track. (*There are a lot of wayside crosses in this section.*) At road in **Les Albusquiès** turn R and 50m later turn L downhill, L again, veer R and KSO(R) down grassy walled lane downhill continuing between fields to road (1.5km). Turn L (*picnic area to R below*) and 500m later, at junction at top of hill, turn R (signed 'Espeyrac', *good views if clear*). Continue on road, zigzagging down through hamlets of **Campagnac** (593m), **Le Soulié** (*Gîte-Accueil au Soulié de Saint-Jacques, 05.65.72.90.18 & 06.80.00.32.52, 7pl, April–Oct, donation*) and **Carboniés**. Continue L on road then, at bend, fork R onto FP through woods (**Camin d'Olt**) downhill again. KSO(R) at fork shortly afterwards, follow track round, cross bridge over river, veering L at fork on other side. Continue on walled lane, turn L onto small street at entrance to Espeyrac and reach road by Mairie, church and gîte d'étape in...

8.5km Espeyrac 369m (190.5/547.5)

Hotel/bar/restaurant, café, shop (behind hotel), fountain/♣ by church. Gîte d'étape communal behind Mairie (05.65.72.93.46 or 05.65.69.88.69, 12pl, 1/4–31/10, K).

Church of Saint Pierre has almost life-size statue of Saint-Roch pilgrim on L inside and also unusual statue of St Peter with a cockerel at his feet (on R inside).

Turn L, follow road round side of church to small square with restored well then turn hard R, passing shop and hotel. Cross road and KSO on other side down road leading to cemetery, pass to L of it and continue on FP to cross FB over the river. Turn L on other side up FP winding its way uphill to minor road 800m later at staggered junction with wayside cross. KSO ahead and then KSO(L) at U-bend in another road. About 100m later fork L down grassy track, cross river again by new footbridge and turn R along D42 for 510m to hamlet of **Célis**. Turn L and then R up RH side of farm and KSO(R) up steep shady FP (> walled lane) and continue uphill; pass cemetery and enter village of…

3.5km Sénergues 506m (194/544)

Hotel, 3 bar-restaurants, bakery, PTT and other shops. Private *gîte d'étape* in Domaine de Sénos, large house on LH side of road at entry to village (05.65.72.91.56, 33pl, 15/3–15/11, K). Picnic area with ♣ by church and pilgrim shelter (with ♣) on leaving village. Church of St Martin (statue of St Roch pilgrim inside on back wall, nice modern stained-glass windows) on site of 9th-century priory. Tour Carré.

Turn R up narrow lane to church *(shady square at side is a good place for a rest, good views)*. Pass church, turn L down main street and KSO(L) to end of village. Just after petrol pumps turn R up narrow FP by bus shelter and electricity transformer, cross road at top and KSO uphill up gravel lane. KSO ahead up another road at top, passing 'Abris Pèlerins' on L *(with WC, picnic seating, sink and wash basins, all under cover)*. Enter woods, climbing steeply all the time (this is the **Forêt Départementale de Sénergues**). Veer L on lane alongside edge of woods *(fields to R)* and track begins to level out.

On leaving woods KSO(L) along lane, undulating between fields. KSO until you reach road, turn L, 20m before five-way junction with D42 and D137 *(large modern wooden wayside cross)*. If you are tired or the weather is bad you can continue straight ahead on the D42, picking up the GR65 again 1.5km later (marked*, not much traffic) after it has done a 'loop'.

Turn R (at junction) along D137 for 750m and at RH bend turn L onto grassy lane along ridge between fields. Descend through woods to join unsurfaced track coming from back R and fork L almost immediately afterwards along grassy track through fields to rejoin D42*. Turn R (not much traffic) and KSO for 2km, almost level, on a ridge-like road with splendid views, until you come to the junction above the hamlet of…

5km Fontromieu 591m (199/539)

Here the D42 turns L but you KSO along minor road to…

1km Saint-Marcel 570m (200/538) ♣

Church of Saint-Marcel (a pope, martyred in 309), but nothing is left of the original Romanesque building except the chapel; the present church was rebuilt in 1561 but only finally finished in 1875. The statue of St Roch as a pilgrim, with hat, scallops, stick and gourd (that was inside the church when a previous edition of this guide was being prepared), seems to have disappeared. Stained-glass window above door has three scallop shells. There was a leprosarium here in the 17th and 18th centuries and a Chapelle St Roch built in 1629, at the height of the plague. This is the original pilgrim route, which ran along the ridge before descending to Conques in the valley below.

Leave Saint-Marcel and continue on ridge road for 1.5km to isolated farm at the *lieu-dit* **La Croix Torte**, a five-point junction at a place where several sets of telegraph poles and wires intersect. Turn L steeply downhill on gravel lane as far as a pair of gates, then pass to RH side of them down shady, narrow rocky walled lane, descending all the time. Path gradually widens out as you go. Reach a road on the outskirts of **Conques**, cross over to take *second* RH turn (cul-de-sac sign). KSO(L) at fork down pedestrianised **Rue Emile Rondié** and at next fork either KSO(R) on level for municipal gîte d'étape or KSO(L) downhill for abbey.

3km Conques 280m (203/535)

Two hotels, 4 CH, shop, bakery, restaurants, post office + ATM, TO (Rue du Chanoine Benazech). Accueil Abbaye Sainte-Foy (Communauté des Prémontrés) in abbey has dormitory accommodation for pilgrims plus rooms (05.65.69.85.12, 96pl, open all year, phone ahead). Gîte d'étape communal, Rue Emile Roudié, in former gendarmerie (05.65.72.82.98, 35pl, April–Oct, K), gîte d'étape Le Gîte du Frayssou, Rue Emile Roudié (05.81.19.90.21 & 06.15.35.17.68, 6pl, May–June and Sept, K). Camping Beau Rivage by river (Mar–Oct). ▶

Conques cathedral

Conques cathedral, detail of tympanum (Photo: Marigold Fox)

The whole town is a historic monument so the *balises* are very discreet: wooden squares, carved, so watch out carefully for them. Abbey church (cathedral) of Sainte-Foy (Saint Faith): its origins date from the 8th century though the present-day building is from the 11th. Tympanum of the Last Judgement scene on the main doorway is a very fine example of Romanesque sculpture and the abbey also has a medieval treasury. The abbey became famous when the remains of Sainte-Foy (martyred in AD303 and famous for her ability to cure eye disorders) were brought here from the church on the outskirts of Agen (where she came from and was buried) by one Arivisius, a monk from Conques. He had apparently spent several years in Agen with the religious community whose duty it was to guard her remains. Gradually he gained their confidence, until one day an opportunity arose to steal the casket containing them and take them back with him to Conques. Here the relics attracted enormous numbers of pilgrims and led to the expansion of the church to accommodate them.

From the church, fork L down the **Rue Charlemagne** *(paved)* and continue downhill, under the **Porte du Barry**. Pass turning (L) up to **Chapelle Saint-Roch** *(perched up on top of hill above L, good views back over Conques in evening sunlight)* and continue steeply down to the bottom of the hill. Cross the road and continue across old pilgrim bridge over the **Dourdou**. On other side continue on road for 200m then KSO ahead up FP through woods, climbing steeply. Cross road and continue uphill on other side to…

1.5km Chapelle Sainte-Foy (204.5/533.5)

Site of a local pilgrimage, chapel built by a spring whose waters were reputed to be miraculous cures for eye complaints. Modern stained-glass window of St James as pilgrim inside. View of Conques.

Continue on FP, climbing until you come out onto a ridge. Then, at a junction of similar tracks 1.5km after the chapel, the GR65 divides into the *main route* and the *variante* (both waymarked):

a) What is now the main route is, in fact, another 'scenic detour', 5km longer than the more direct *variante* and involves 900m of *dénivélés* (changes of height). It is also less pilgrim-oriented as it misses out the Chapelle Saint-Roch and the Stations of the Cross leading up to it. Turn R here if you want to take this option *(in exceptionally fine weather as it has good views)*. b) For the *variante* route via Noailhac KSO ahead alongside fence and 150m later turn L onto a minor road. KSO along it for 1km until you reach a junction with the D606 and turn L along it. KSO for 1.5km to junction with D580; turn hard L on it then veer R and KSO into village of…

4km Noailhac (208.5/529.5)

Gîte d'étape communal, 100m before village (05.65.72.91.25, 18pl, all year, K). Café-restaurant-shop Chemin Saint-Jacques with CH (05.65.72.91.25 & 06.79.29.59.44).

Pass church of **Saint-Jean-Baptiste** *(restored in 17th century on site of 15th-century building)* and at junction continue straight ahead uphill (marked 'Decazeville'). Then, when road veers L, KSO(R) up lane (signposted 'La Merlaterie' and 'Chapelle St Roch'). Pass 13 large wayside crosses (track continues as a walled lane after no. 4), forming a *Via Crucis* (Stations of the Cross – no 14, the last, is next to the chapel), leading up to the D580 at the…

Modern stained-glass St James, Chapelle Sainte-Foy

Map 6: Noailhac to Figeac

3km Chapelle Saint-Roch 595m (211.5/526.5)

Picnic area; splendid views looking over Conques in valley below. The chapel has statue of saint as a pilgrim outside in the tympanum above the door and another (as a non-pilgrim) inside above the altar. The chapel is the focus of a local annual pilgrimage on 16 August, St Roch's Day; this began between 1847–9 when, due to a typhoid epidemic, a procession of local people made its way to the top of the hill, where public prayers were addressed to the saint, invoking his help. As a result the number of those inflicted with the disease is reported to have decreased rapidly and the custom has continued ever since. The chapel was built on the site in 1884. It also contains two modern stained-glass windows, donated by the artist in 1997 and 2000.

Continue on road for 500m, uphill, to TV mast (640m) and very large wayside cross. *Panoramic views and orientation plan.*

KSO (road descends after TV mast), and at five-point junction 3km after Noailhac KSO on D580 (marked 'Decazeville'). About 300m after turning to **Fonteilles** fork L up sandy lane. *(Noticeboard at start explains the* Méridienne verte, *the line North Pole–Paris–South Pole, which was planted with a line of trees in 2000 to mark the millenium.)* KSO, with fence to L, through fields, then descending gradually down side of hillside with valley below you to LH side. Cross a minor road and continue on grassy track on other side. *(View of Decazeville ahead; the big scar on the landscape to your L is the remains of the opencast coal mine.)* About 200m later track splits: KSO to *R-hand* side of fence, heading for woods ahead. Go through small gate and just before you reach the woods fork L down FP leading downhill to large green industrial building on RH side. Continue ahead on gravel track and KSO(L) ahead behind farm buildings, downhill all the time. Reach a road coming from back R and KSO along it.

At junction *(***Le Plegat**, *gîte d'étape at Le Buscalie indicated ahead at entrance to cul-de-sac)* KSO on road, veering R. At junction by farm (**Fromentals**) fork L downhill, descending steadily all the time. Pass **La Gaillardie** and then **La Combe** *(seat).* Pass entrance to **Le Madieu** (on L) but KSO(R) on road ahead. At fork *(with seat, picnic area,* ♣ *)* KSO(R) ahead (**Route de Vivioles**). At end of this KSO ahead on **Route de Montarnal** and continue downhill all the time, through residential area, and reach road with a 'stop' sign (**Avenue Marméjours**, *bar opposite*) on the outskirts of…

Chapelle Saint-Roch, near Noailhac

11km Decazeville 225m (222.5/515.5)

Medium-sized town (population 7000) with all facilities, hotel, TO (Square Jean Segalat). Gite d'Etape Les Volets Bleus, 3 Rue Camille Douls (on GR65, 05.65.64.49.05 & 06.72.19.64.48, 17pl, 1/4–15/10, K, SNCF. (If you intend to sleep in Livinhac on a Monday buy food here.)

The town takes its present name from the Duc de Decazes, Minister of Industry under Napoleon and responsible for the promotion of large-scale mining in this area. Decazeville had the largest opencast coalmine in Europe, La Découverte (visits possible).

Turn L first then R (**Rue Camille Douls**, Gîte 'Les Volets Bleus' at no. 3), then at traffic lights turn R uphill (**Avenue Laromiguère**, but unmarked at start, house no. 13 has sign 'eau potable' outside). Turn R at traffic lights and then 20m later turn L up steep hill (**Route de Nantuech**) which turns R 200m later up very steep hill, veering L and climbing continuously. At the top road levels out and at end of village (**Nantuech**) KSO(R) along road joining from L *(wayside cross and seat)*. About 100m later turn hard L *(***Chemin de Boutigou***, uphill again!)* and KSO, emerging at staggered junction *(another wayside cross and seat)* in a residential area. KSO ahead (still on **Chemin de Boutigou**). Pass cemetery (L) and reach…

2km Eglise Saint-Roch 353m (224.5/513.5)

Small Accueil Chrétien, 'le Dioscore', in former convent opposite church (06.88.93.74.33, 7pl, donations).

A parish church, rather than the usual chapel or hermitage dedicated to this saint. Three statues of him inside the church, one above the main altar in full pilgrim gear, another large statue as pilgrim but minus hat in side chapel and a third small (alabaster?) statue of the saint as a non-pilgrim at the side of the altar in the side chapel. There is also a modern drawing of St Roch the pilgrim walking with his dog by his side in front of the chapel at Noailhac, but here his cloak is down and his wound covered up as he is on the move.

KSO on D157 for 1km then turn R down grassy lane opposite farm in **Pomayrols**, veering L and descending steadily all the time, zigzagging down to the D21 opposite the modern bridge over the **Lot** at the entrance to…

2km Livinhac-le-Haut 220m (226.5/511.5)

Café, bakery, shop, post office, ♣ by Mairie. Gîte d'étape communal, Place du 14 Juin by church, (06.76.86.94.77, 22pl, 15/3–31/10, K). Accueil pèlerin, La Magnanerie, 170 Rue du Faubourg, CH/mini-gîte (05.65.43.25.56, phone ahead). 2 CH: a) la Coquille Bleue, 25 Rue Camille Couderc (05.65.43.39.52 & 06.65.79.39.56 and b) Impasse des Esplagnes (05.65.63.36.97 & 06.72.07.64.03). Camping le Roquelongue by river at entrance to town (all year, restaurant-bar, rents caravans per night).

Cross bridge and turn first L up long street (**Rue Camille Couderc**, *but no name at start*), cross a more major road and fork L ahead (**Rue de la République**) to **Place du 14 Juin**.

Cross square and go down **Rue Camille Landes** to R of Mairie. Turn into **Rue du Couderc** and continue to road junction (D627 and D21). Cross over and go down D627 (signed 'Capdenac'). About 300m later, in hamlet of **La Planque**, fork R by wayside cross and 20m later on, at farm building, KSO ahead up narrow lane to minor road junction (**Peyrols**, *seat, gîte to L)*).

KSO up road, ignoring turns, to hamlet of **Le Thabor** and then turn hard R at bend down gravelled lane. When this veers R, KSO(L) ahead along grassy lane to road junction (marked 'Le Poux', 'Chaunac') ahead. *Gîte Les Monts de Chaunac 400m off route here (05.65.43.58.34 & 06.37.88.52.19, 11pl, all year, K)*. Turn L along D21 and 50m later turn R up minor road (marked 'Le Feydel'). About 150m later turn L up tarred lane marked 'Le Feydel' and 100m later turn R up grassy lane for 100m to farm at U-bend in minor road. KSO(L) ahead, uphill, *then along ridge)*. About 800m later join minor road coming from back R then turn L onto D2 *(picnic area with ♣)* at entrance to...

6km Montredon 396m (232.5/505.5)

♣ CH 'La Mariotte' on GR 65 on leaving village (05.65.34.38.20, 15/3–15/11).
    Hilltop village with Chapelle Notre-Dame at crossroads (replaces older chapel has 14th century *pieta* above altar) and Church of Saint-Michel on site of former priory (AP in room at back of church). You are now in the *département* of the Lot.

Turn R on D2 and continue uphill to church. Veer L past it and continue downhill on road, turn R at junction (pass 'La Mariotte' on L and 200m later, at staggered junction, KSO ahead uphill. Turn L 100m later (marked 'Tournié'), following road round through hamlet of **Tournié** and KSO ahead at crossroads, downhill.

Turn L into hamlet of **Lacoste** *(note well on L)*, continue down unsurfaced road and 200m later turn R downhill on green lane. Turn L at bottom onto road and L again at fork. About 200m later on at road junction reach…

3km Chapelle de Guirande 277m (235.5/502.5)

Romanesque chapel of Sainte-Madeleine with late 14th-century murals of the four evangelists over altar (in good condition). *Gîte d'étape/equestre* and *camping à la ferme* at Le Communal (400m away to L, 05.65.50.10.45, 25pl, Easter–1/11).

Turn R and pass to RH side of cemetery ♣ to road.

*From here the GR65 does quite a few 'loops' to avoid the road, something made more difficult by numerous tracks in private ownership, so from here to Saint-Félix those in a hurry or in bad weather may prefer to continue on the D2 from the chapel (3km) instead of taking the (6km) 'scenic route' via a reservoir and various green lanes, some of which may well be very boggy. Turn L for Saint-Félix when you get to **La Ragoulie**.*

The GR65 turns R again 100m after the chapel up a minor road to hamlet of **Guirande**. At T-junction turn R down lane lined with oak trees, which then turns L onto track at small aerodrome. KSO(L) along side of fields downhill to road. KSO then turn first L downhill by wayside cross in hamlet of **Le Terly**, leading down to reservoir *(plan d'eau)*. Cross it by a causeway, KSO ahead on other side, passing to L of farm, and continue ahead, downhill along line of trees. Around 300/400m later turn L down similar track. Continue on road (in hamlet of **Bord**, *CH, 05.65.10.66.71 & 06.18.62.25.24*) and turn R. At end of hamlet veer R down grassy lane, then L, then R onto fenced-in lane leading to road in hamlet of **La Cipière**. KSO(R) along it to road (D2, *watch out here for new rerouted FP direct to the church in Saint-Félix*) and after 300m turn hard R at junction (V9) along road for 1km to…

6km Saint-Félix (241.5/496.5)

Auberge campagnarde (midday meals if pre-booked, 05.65.50.14.01 but check opening hours). Romanesque church of Sainte-Radegonde has Adam and Eve with tree and serpent on its 11th-century tympanum. Early 20th century stained-glass window of St James.

Saint-Félix, Church of Sainte-Radegonde, tympanum with Adam and Eve

Fork L after church (behind restaurant), passing between buildings onto a narrow FP. At top (**Le Puech**, bend in road to L) turn R along tree-lined lane to road. KSO(R) along it then turn L at crossroads. About 100m later turn R up grassy lane then KSO up minor road. Turn R at next junction uphill to road in hamlet of **La Causse**. Turn L at top and 80m later, just before village entrance boards for St-Jean Mirabel fork R (opposite fire hydrant) down lane leading to D2. Cross over and KSO ahead on other side then, at staggered junction, turn L past *salle communale* (on L) with a sculpture of an enormous bicycle outside.

*Turn R here for 200m (and then retrace your steps) to visit the **Eglise de Saint-Jean Mirabel** – Romanesque, recently restored. Framed painting of a very sturdy-looking Saint Roch (with stick, dog and bread) inside on R. A modern stained-glass pilgrim window (above the altar) has a rucksack, stick and gourd while the tympanum frieze over the west door (the original entrance to the church when it was still only a chapel) dates from the 13th century and depicts scenes concerning St John the Evangelist in the top row and St Jean the Baptist in the lower row of sculptures.*

Turn R onto the D2 at the end and KSO. At brow of hill by RH bend (place marked on map as **Bel-Air**) fork L down walled lane to road. Turn L for 80m then R (marked 'Les Crouzets' and 'L'Hôpital'), and 300m later turn R up green lane.

Saint-Jean Mirabel, bicycle sculpture outside salle communale

Emerge onto gravel lane and KSO(R) to D2 by junction, turn L and then L again to D210 *(leading to* **Lunan**, *1km, whose church of St Martin is a historic monument, 200m)*. Turn R down tarred road 1200m later, at entrance to **La Balme**, which > an unsurfaced track, descending to crossing of paths, the…

4.5km Carrefour des Sentiers 327m (246/492)

Turn R up green lane, veering L and rising slowly up to road 800m later. Turn R for 150m to D2 then turn L *(view of Figeac ahead)*. About 100m later fork L, KSO(L) at fork and 800m later reach the junction with the GR6A just after the *lieu-dit* **Pipy**. Turn R for Figeac here *(see below)*, opposite a farm (**Fournamantane**).

Here you have the option of a) continuing ahead here straight to **La Cassagnole** *(gîte d'étape) via the GR6A, picking up the GR65 again after the Aiguille du Cingle (an obelisk) or b) turning R to go into* **Figeac**.

a) To go directly to **La Cassagnole** *(with green walker symbols)* KSO ahead for 150m, then turn R at junction onto another minor road. At the *next* junction,

300m later, turn R *(turn L for Centre Leclerc with large superstore: food, cafeteria and ATM)*. Continue ahead, cross D840 *(new roundabout layout)* and continue on other side marked 'Fumat' *(café/restaurant on corner)*. KSO ahead then 800m later fork L up grassy track with high(ish) wall to LH side.

Cross minor road (water tower to R) and KSO on walled lane. Cross another minor road (follow *green* signs here as GR6A turns R here) and KSO ahead along another walled lane, veering R to D922. Turn L along it and 250m later turn L (before roundabout sign) along minor road (signed R to 'L'Aiguille' and 'Monument du Cingle') and the GR65 from Figeac joins at next crossing from R below *(obelisk and shady picnic area with ♣)*. Turn L here, veering R along boundary wall and fence to a roundabout *(waymarks with a yellow walker on a green background)*. Cross over, go down D822 for 100m then fork R (marked for 'La Cassagnole') past factories in an industrial estate. After bend in road fork R down minor road marked 'Z.I. Aiguille' and continue as described below* (see page 99).

b) To go into **Figeac** turn R here down walled lane *(dovecote to L)*. At field at end turn L down walled FP, skirting it, and KSO. Cross track and KSO downhill to D2 and turn L down to junction with N140. Cross it (carefully) and 20m later turn L up green lane and then R along road, uphill, // to N140 (to your L below). KSO(L) along road coming from back R and descend to cross railway line. Continue down **Rue de Londrieu**. Turn L along **Allées Victor Hugo**, then R and either KSO and cross bridge over the river to visit Figeac or turn L immediately down **Avenue Jean-Jaurès** to continue on GR65.

5km Figeac 194m (251/487)

All facilities. SNCF (Paris, Brive, Toulouse), 7 hotels. 10 restaurants, TO (Hôtel de la Monnaie, Place Vival). Gîte/CH Le Soleilho, 8 Rue du Prat (05.65.34.64.41 & 06.79.13.00.70, 6pl, all year, K). CH Les Pratges, 6 Avenue Jean-Jaurès (05.65.50.01.42 & 06.07.05.07.92). Camping-Restaurant Les Rives du Célé, Domaine du Surgié (April–Sept).

Busy town on river Célé (population 10,500) with network of restored medieval streets (ask in TO for walking tour leaflet), worth half a day's visit. Former abbey church of Saint-Sauveur, consecrated 1093, with ambulatory characteristic of pilgrim churches. Churches of Notre-Dame du Puy and Saint Thomas. Formerly an important pilgrim halt with six hospitals (one still exists). Newly renovated Musée Champollion (Egyptology), Musée du Vieux Figeac, Gothic Hôtel de la Monnaie, Maison des Templiers.

SECTION 2
Figeac to Moissac

To continue: turn L down **Avenue Jean-Jaurès**. About 150m later turn (second) L up street (marked 'Cingles Bas') alongside high wall, veering R then L under railway line. Turn R and then fork L uphill. Road > forest track through woods, climbing steadily up side of hill and veering L, passing TV mast to reach war memorial, *an enormous concrete cross, with the names of the 145 people deported on 12 May 1944. Picnic area with view over town of Figeac.*

Continue ahead on road, mainly uphill, for 1.5km to second monument *(obelisks marking limits of 8th-century Benedictine abbey, another picnic area)*: this is the place where the *GR65A* variante *meets up with the GR65 again*.*

To continue on GR65, turn R (the waymarks ahead are those of the GR65A). About 200m later KSO(R) along D922 and 100m later fork R down wide road past factories and marked 'Z.I. Aiguille'.

KSO along level road on ridge, ignoring turns to L and R. *(On the skyline you can see the water tower in Faycelles as a reference point.)*

KSO(R) at next junction and continue along road, passing **Malaret**, passing above **Buffan** and just after a crossroads KSO to...

5km La Cassagnole 311m (256/482)
Birthplace of Louis the Pious, son of Charlemagne and second Holy Roman Emperor. Gîte d'Etape Relais Saint-Jacques, 05.65.34.03.08, 33pl, all year, K, limited food supplies for sale, also CH).

KSO(R) at fork and continue on road through **Ferrières**, KSO(L) at junction *(with modern stone cross)*. KSO(R) at next junction *(note dovecote to R)*. Join road from back L *(another dovecote to R)*. Cross D662 and continue into village, veering R uphill to church in...

4km Faycelles 319m (260/478)
Bar/restaurant/shop 'La Forge' with CH (on main street, 05.65.34.65.09).

Continue ahead L, past church, uphill, KSO(L) up walled lane at bend, reach D21 and turn R along it. *(Viewpoint with picnic tables. Good view over Lot valley.)* KSO(R) at junction.

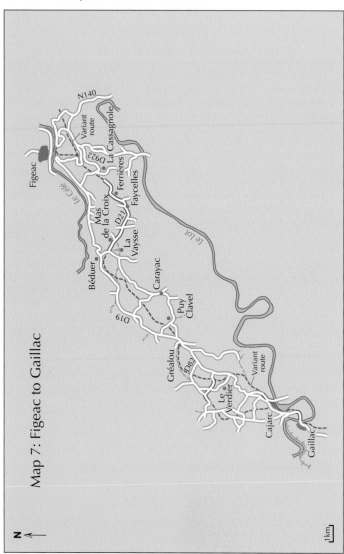

Map 7: Figeac to Gaillac

Note caselles *in this area. Also steeply pitched barns, two storeys, with grassy ramp leading up to first-floor entrance.*

Continue on D21 for 2km until just past RH turn for *Ayrens (hard R, Restaurant Le Bar de l'Eté, open 11:00–15:00 Sat, May–September)*, then fork L down shady lane (to side of bar/restaurant) for 300m to road. *(200m ahead on L is La Planquette, a gîte d'étape, 05.65.40.01.36, 10pl + 8 in marquee in summer, campsite, April–Sept).* Turn R and then R again almost immediately down FP and at end turn R onto D18 just before its junction with the D21 in hamlet of…

3.5km Mas de la Croix 327m (263.5/474.5)

This is where the GR651 starts, the (waymarked) variante *route along the Vallée du Célé: see Appendix C.*

a) *For GR651:* KSO on D21 to **Béduer** *(0.8km, bakery + limited groceries, two bar/restaurants, CH 05.65.11.40.86 & 06.88.21.13.00, K, camping).*

b) *For GR65:* fork L by bus shelter down minor road, pass above château and then, at small crossing *(base of stone wayside cross to R)* turn L up narrow walled lane which then > a minor road. When it bends R downhill turn L down a (wider) walled lane and KSO, ignoring turns, as it wends its way downhill *(large lavoir/fountain, the Fontieu, to R)* and then up to minor road.

Two-storey barn, typical of the Lot

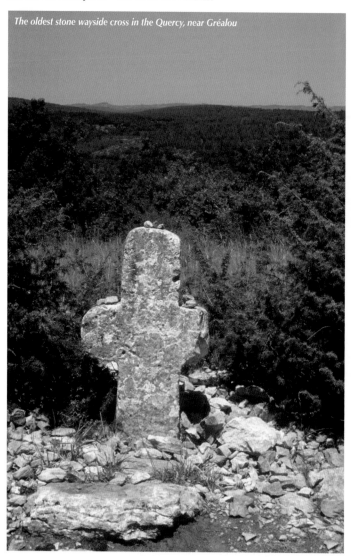

The oldest stone wayside cross in the Quercy, near Gréalou

Turn L and immediately R uphill at junction (marked 'Surgues') then turn L down gravel track 150m later at bend and KSO *(note caselle/gaviote to L)*, ignoring turns. When it > a walled lane (farm of **Combes-Salgues** to L) KSO. At crossing of paths 100m later turn R for 2km along another walled lane.

KSO, ignoring turns, to road (D38). Turn L for 300m then turn R down track. KSO. In a grassy clearing where track forks L fork R up grassy lane. KSO ahead at crossing and continue uphill to road in hamlet of **Le Puy Clavel** *New 24pl gîte and CH on GR itself (Ecoasis, 06.71.00.48.30, meals available, K)*. Turn R and 100m later turn L down grassy track. KSO to road, veering L to a walled lane, and turn R uphill to D19 *(Gréalou place-name boards to L)*. Cross over and KSO *(large iron cross to L)*.

In this area the footpaths are often broken by roads/staggered junctions/short stretches on road, hence the complicated instructions.

Turn hard L 300m later after waterworks building, then R at junction and arrive at the church in...

9km Gréalou 374m (272.5/465.5)

Hotel/bar/restaurant des Quatre Vents (not always open). CH Atelier des Volets Bleus, Place de l'Eglise (05.65.40.69.86 & 06.84.37.64.73, 6pl). CH next to hotel (05.65.40.66.00 & 06.07.09.59.85). ♣ in picnic area. Romanesque church of Notre-Dame de l'Assomption. There are a lot of dolmens in this area.

Turn R at church, pass cemetery (R) and continue on lane. At junction with road and small iron cross KSO(L) ahead on track along ridge, continuing along open heathland to small stone cross *(thought to be the oldest such cross in the region)*. Opposite a dolmen veer L down green lane alongside wall and continue down to road (D82) and KSO on other side down walled lane, ignoring turnings. KSO ahead at junction and continue until you reach a road. Turn R and then at a T-junction turn R again to hamlet of...

4km Le Verdier 316m (276.5/461.5)

In bad weather you may want to take the variant route through the woods to Cajarc *(2km shorter, via the GR65A, waymarked)*. If so KSO on here on road then turn L onto a minor road leading to the D21. KSO(R) then KSO along it for 1km. Then, just before the junction with the D19, fork R onto path. Turn R on D19 and 50m later turn L onto wide gravel path. KSO, following it round, and at T-junction with similar paths, turn R. Follow track down for 2km and at T-junction at very bottom turn R ('no entry' sign). Tarmac at first then grassy FP downhill. Cross tarred lane and KSO on other side (**Chemin de la Salle**). Reach a bigger road* marked 'Centre Ville 400m' to R and turn R here. When you reach the **Boulevard de la Tour de la Ville** turn R to the **Place du Forail** in the centre of **Cajarc**.

*Note: the GR *variante* continues ahead here (still the **Chemin de la Salle**), goes under the railway line, turns R along the river and then rejoins the main GR65 but without taking you into the town centre.

Otherwise, to continue on the main GR65, turn R into hamlet and KSO on road, uphill for 500m, to crossroads *(iron cross)*. KSO ahead (marked 'Chemin des Vignes'), continuing to climb until you reach another road. Turn L and 150m later fork L up unsurfaced road and KSO through fields, track then becoming a green lane. At crossing KSO ahead (level) and continue to road. Cross over and continue on other side on track which > walled lane, descending until you reach a T-junction with ruined building on L.

Dolmen, near Gréalou

Turn L along track and KSO, ignoring turns, uphill to road. Cross it and continue ahead down green lane, descending to join road coming from back L. KSO(R) for 20m then KSO(L) (at bend to R in road) down walled lane. This > a tarred lane, descending all the time.

About 150m after road joins from back R turn R along green lane under the cliffs *(Cajarc below L)*. This > a stony track that descends continuously in a straight line until you reach a field at the bottom. Turn R alongside a wall on a grassy path and then KSO along minor road at end and turn L onto D922.

The GR65 does not enter Cajarc either. *To visit town:* KSO. *To continue:* turn R immediately (after turning L onto D922).

6km Cajarc 160m (282.5/455.5)

All facilities. TO (Place du Forail). Gîte d'étape communal, Place du Forail (06.14.66.54.89, 20pl, March–November, K + 16 pl in 2 large tents on municipal campsite, beds, K, May–Sept), Gîte d'Etape Le Pèlerin, 11 Rue Lacauhne (05.65.40.65.31 & 06.74.32.44.40, 23pl, April–Oct, K, also CH). Gîte, 8 Impasse des Lilas (05.65.40.61.00 & 06.30.65.43.26, 3pl, all year). 4 other CH, 3 hotels. Camping municipal du Terriol (on GR out of town, May–Sept).

Town situated in a 'circus' of chalk cliffs. Pilgrim bridge over the Lot built in 1320 and a hospital existed in 1269. Chapelle de la Madeleine (only the chancel remains, known as 'Chapelette de Cajarc' today, the chapel of former 13th-century leprosarium).

Note: After Gaillac the causse begins, with no food or water until Cahors, except in Limogne and Varaire, so stock up on both before leaving Cajarc.

To leave from town centre (**Place du Forail**, facing TO) turn L, continue on **Boulevard de la Tour de Ville** and turn R into **Avenue de la Capalette** then 2nd L into **Rue de Cuzoul**, picking up the waymarks again, and KSO past campsite. Continue alongside railway line (on LH side) and just before *second* tunnel underneath it turn R along side of garden and then L up stony FP to road *(D922, above R under cliffs)*. KSO(L) ahead and then KSO(L) again at junction with the 'Capelette' *(on L, 11th and 15th centuries)* and huge wooden cross (on R). *Picnic area.*

KSO(L) here (**Chemin de la Route Veille**) and fork R 100m later. KSO(R) and after 1km *(CH on GR itself, partway down on R, 1.5km after Cajarc, 05.65.40.70.00 & 06.24.11.11.69, April to October, K)* and descend to five-way junction. Take second R *(brickworks to R. Note very large cages on L, used for drying corn on the cob)* then join D19 (**Route de Limogne**) coming from back R.

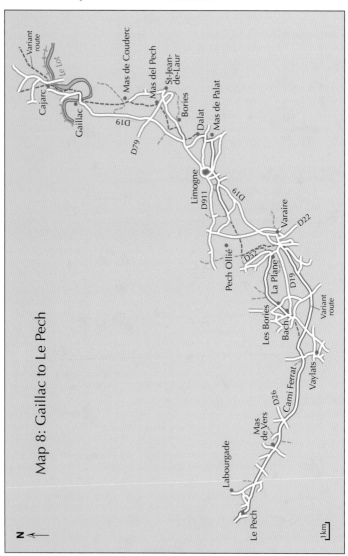

Map 8: Gaillac to Le Pech

(Church in Gaillac up on clifftop ahead of you.) Cross suspension bridge over the **Lot** and turn L on other side, continuing uphill on road to entry to...

4km Gaillac 180km (286.5/451.5)

Gîte (on RH side of road, take staircase 30m after sign for 'Gaillac' 05.65.40.66.18, April–Oct, K).

At RH bend on entry to village fork L steeply up short FP and KSO(L) up minor road, KSO(L) at fork and continue ahead on level grassy lane. At junction KSO(L) on track from back R and enter woods, uphill, veering L. KSO(R) at fork and then fork R again (the centre of three) almost immediately, continuing on stony track. *(Watch out carefully for waymarks as there are no distinguishing features in the* cause *and no views through or over the trees, which are not very tall and mostly old and untended.)*

Turn L at crossing near brow of hill and KSO ahead along track coming from back L. KSO along track coming from back R and fork L almost immediately afterwards. KSO, mainly uphill, then ahead at crossing. Reach minor tarred road coming from back L and KSO(R) along it, uphill, passing the entrance gates (L) to **Mas de Couderc** (a farm) some 700m later. Pass turning (L) to Salvagnac and Cajarc on bigger road and KSO(R) ahead; then, by wayside cross, fork R down grassy track which > a walled lane. Track joins from back R; KSO. Reach large pond surrounded by stone wall and pass to R of it (♣). Turn R onto road, reach junction with wayside cross and continue ahead on tarred lane on other side. KSO(L) in hamlet of...

6km Mas del Pech 339m (292.5/445.5)

KSO ahead down narrow walled lane. About 1km later reach T-junction with wider walled lane and turn R and then fork L 50m later. Follow lane round for 1km, veering L by farm and reach road *(lavoir L, another pond surrounded by stone walls, waterlilies R)* in hamlet of...

2km Mas de Borie (294.5/443.5)

Turn R. Continue ahead on road for 1km, pass wayside cross (L) and KSO. At T-junction and bend turn L up small shady walled lane, gradually uphill. Near top turn R, veering L, to very minor tarred lane by entrance to farm (**Mas de Teule**). Turn R.

KSO(R) uphill at T-junction and reach another T-junction with wayside cross in hamlet of **Mas de Dalat**. Turn L, veering R 50m later, then turn R at bend 100m after that onto walled lane, veering L up into woods. About 300–400m later turn L at junction, gently downhill, and shortly afterwards reach the D143 and turn L along it uphill into **Mas de Palat**.

Fork L onto tarred lane, turn hard R (turn L for CH 'La Hulotte') and KSO ahead at fork past iron cross. Continue on raised path between fields, veering L uphill on shady walled lane. Similar track joins from back R; KSO ahead on shady walled lane. Continue ahead (**Chemin de Malecargue**) *(this is also a* sentier botanique, *with labels on plants and bushes to either side of it)*. Reach a road, KSO along it and then turn R 50m later *(wayside cross)*, gently downhill through residential area *(shady seat to R)* to junction of D911 and D19 at entry to town. Turn L along it, passing gîte d'étape 100m later on RH side of road and continue into the centre of…

6km Limogne-en-Quercy 300m (300.5/437.5)

Small town with shops, cafés, restaurant, TO 55 Place d'Occitaine. Gîte d'étape communal, Route de Villefranche (06.12.84.86.47, 19pl, all year, K). Gîte d'Etape Les Gloriettes, 60 Route de Cahors, opposite bank, on leaving town, 06.26.86.37.94, 15pl, April to September, K). Camping municipal Bel-Air on edge of town (on D911, April–September).

Lavoir outside Limogne

To leave: watch out carefully for the waymarking as the GR65 has now been rerouted to go through the town (rather than skirt it). Leave on the D19 and then continue ahead on a wide walled lane, semi-shaded, for 2km, descending gradually to road just before farm in **Ferrières**. Turn R and continue uphill, then fork L at junction with wayside cross. About 150m later KSO(R) down walled lane (another farm to L) and 500m later, as you begin to descend, turn R through a *cledo* onto FP through trees.

Watch out carefully for waymarks throughout this section; it is easy to be lulled into a rhythm and forget to pay attention.

Around 100m later go through a second *cledo* and turn L along narrow walled lane. After 500m cross road and continue on wider walled lane on other side. After 1km reach another road coming from R *(turn R for gîte équestre at Pech Olié; 900m)*. Continue on road for 75m then continue straight ahead, taking LH of two green lanes at LH bend in road. About 200m later turn L into similar lane and KSO for 1.5km to junction with minor road. Turn R (on road, not hard R on track) and after 200m reach…

6.5km Junction near Varaire (307/431)

Here you have a choice of routes, depending on whether or not you want to go into **Varaire** (eg to sleep) and/or take the variante along *Cami Gasco* (an old Roman road) or bypass it and continue on the main GR65. Both options are way-marked and join up again at the start of the *Cami Ferrat,* 1.5km after **Bach**.

a) To continue on the main GR65: turn R along walled lane for 400m, turn L along road for 200m and fork R up lane. Cross D52 and continue ahead on minor road, meeting the GR36 coming from back L 100m later. Veer L past hamlet of **La Plane** (1km) and KSO(L) down wide unsurfaced track, ignoring turns, for 4km until you reach an isolated house at…

4.5km Les Bories Basses 310m (311.5/426.5)

Continue on minor road. Just after farm the GR65 (KSO) and GR36 separate. KSO for 1km, ignoring turns, to village of…

1km Bach (312.5/425.5)

Restaurant (X Sat & Wed). The village takes its name from a German family who settled here in the 18th century.

Turn R on road (D19, marked 'Caussade'), cross D22 and 600m later fork L down a grassy lane. About 900m later turn R at a junction with a similar track coming from your L, the...

1.5km Junction of the GR65 with its *variante* (314.5/423.5)

b) *The GR65 variante, waymarked, passes to the south of the D19. It takes you along the course of the* Cami Gasco *on wide, almost flat lanes and the occasional minor road and, as explained above, and joins the main GR65 at the start of the section on the* Cami Ferrat *(old Roman road) 1.5km after* **Bach**.

KSO ahead at the junction before **Varaire** and reach the D19 in the centre of the village. *Shop (X Sun pm + all day Mon) and café-restaurant-gîte d'étape Les Marroniers on main road (05.65.31.53.85, 18pl, April–October, K).*

From the D19 (with the bar to your R and the shop to your L) fork L on minor road marked 'M. La Jamblusse', veering L and then fork R at wayside cross up taramac lane. KSO(L) at next junction. KSO ahead, KSO(L) ahead at next fork then, 2km after Varaire, at crossing with an isolated stone building, turn R 2km after that, cross the D22 and continue ahead on other side. KSO, ignoring turns to L and R and 2km later reach the D19. Cross over, KSO ahead on other side and 400m later the main GR65 joins from the RH side at the...

6.5km Junction of the GR65 with its *variante* (314.5/423.5)

Continue ahead and 100m later you reach a junction. *Turn L here if you want to sleep in the gîte run by the nuns in the Monastère des Filles de Jésus in* **Vaylats** *(2.5km, 05.65.31.63.51, open all year, reservation essential). However, to continue the following morning you do not need to backtrack but can turn west along the D19 and after the last house (after the village exit board) a FP is waymarked 'GR,' leading you back onto the* Cami Ferrat *where you turn L.*

Otherwise, KSO ahead. *This is the* Cami Ferrat *('iron path' – it was originally paved) which the GR65 follows for 15km altogether. Like all Roman roads it is more or less straight, and linked Caylus with Cahors. It was not much used by pilgrims in the past, due to its lack of maintenance and its solitude, lending itself readily to ambushes and without easy access either to food or lodging. There are not many distinguishing features in the* causse *it passes through, and few buildings. It is level, in the main, and most of it is either shady or semi-shaded, with woods and/or fields to one side or another. At weekends you may meet people on mountain bikes but on the whole it is a very lonely route, though not as far from habitation, as a glance at a map will reveal, as you might suppose.*

KSO (quite literally!), ignoring turnings, for 7.5km, crossing successively, the D42, the **Ruisseau des Valses** *(a stream that is often dry and where, briefly, the track ceases to be level)* and the D55, reaching the D26 in the hamlet of

7.5km Mas de Vers 252m (322/416)

Cross D26 *(stone cross at junction)*. *Gîte d'étape privé* at **Poudally**, turn L here down D26 *(05.65.22.08.69 & 06.60.09.88.30, 14pl, all year, limited groceries, camping possible)*. The *Cami Ferrat* continues on other side as a minor road. Cross another minor road and the *Cami Ferrat* then > an unsurfaced road. Cross D10 and KSO *(turn L 1km later for Gîte d'Etape Le Gascou, 500m off route, 05.65.31.67.26, 5pl, April–October)*, descending gradually to minor road 1km later at a large *lavoir (good place for rest/shelter in bad weather)*. Turn R shortly before bridge *(signposted for Gîte Privé Elisa at La Boussière (05.65.31.60.46, 4–6pl, April–October, K)*.

6km Junction near Le Pech (328/410)

Turn L along road and KSO to a junction with a minor road *(turn R for 500m up steep hill for* gîte d'étape *at Le Pech, 05.65.24.72.84, 16pl, March–October, K)*. At bend in road KSO ahead on lane, veering L towards road 800m later. Turn hard L uphill then turn R at 'stop' sign, go under motorway and KSO ahead uphill on other side (D6) for 1.5km. At sharp LH bend, at place marked 'Le Gariat', fork R off road onto stony FP uphill. About 250m later, at top of hill, turn R along tarmac lane on ridge, more or less level, then > gravel. KSO for 600m then turn L onto stony track. About 800m after that fork L at intersection of GR65 and GR6, uphill to woods on shady track, levelling out. Pass sports ground/stadium (on R, ♣) and reach junction with C4, just after entrance board for Flaujac-Poujols. Fork L down shady lane, the **Chemin de Saint-Jacques** (or KSO for *Gîte Saint-Antoine, 05.65.20.13.43 or 06.79.84.41.46, 12pl, March–October, K, run by two former pilgrims)*. This is tarred to begin with but > stony FP, down to valley bottom *(passing a fine example of a* caselle *over to L)*. Turn L *(below road)* along valley bottom, gently uphill all the time, for 2km. KSO(R) at fork, then R almost immediately afterwards, on shady path up side of wood. Emerge into the open and pass to RH side of **La Quintade** *(a group of three restored buildings)*, turn R on tarmac lane by its entrance gate, uphill to the D6 in the *lieu-dit* of…

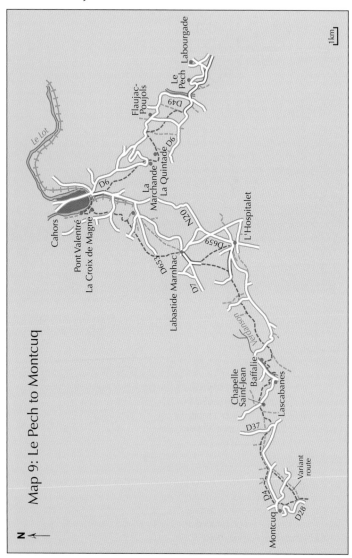

Map 9: Le Pech to Montcuq

N ←

1km

Labourgade
Le Pech
Flaujac-Poujols
D49
Le Lot
D6
La Marchande
La Quintade D6
Cahors
D6
Pont Valentré
La Croix de Magne
N20
L'Hospitalet
D659
D653
Labastide Marnhac
D7
Chapelle Saint-Jean
Baffalie
Vallée du Verdanson
Lascabanes
D37
Montcuq
D4
D28
Variant route

7km La Marchande (335/403)

From here it is nearly all downhill to Cahors. If you want to bypass the town, however, you can turn L here along a 10km *variante* route leading directly to L'Hospitalet (not described here).

Turn R along D6 then fork R along **Route de la Marchande** then turn L down **Chemin de la Marchande**. Reach D6 again, cross over and continue ahead on **Chemin de la Cabridelle**. This then > a track, veering L to open grassland and continuing along a ridge (the **Mont Saint-Georges**).

About 2km later (radio mast to L) track begins to descend. Join minor road coming from back L and KSO. After passing a second radio mast (on L) you can see **Cahors** below for the first time as you begin to descend steeply. Turn R downhill at T-junction, zigzagging down to a railway line (on your L, on **Chemin du Pech de Fourgues**). Then turn L to go under it (the railway) when you reach a more major road which > the **Rue du Barry** *(turn R here for gîte/CH La Maison des Pèlerins, 158 Rue des Cayssine (05.65.30.03.06 & 06.21.10.63.61, phone ahead, 10pl, evening prayers, 12/4–4/10 X 27/6–14/7, after 15:30, K)* in the **Quartier Saint-Georges** in...

5km Cahors 122m (340/398)

All facilities. SNCF (Paris–Toulouse–Port Bou), TO (Place François Mitterand). 10 hotels, 2 Accueils Pèlerins: a) the L'Octroi de Cahors association welcomes pilgrims (almost) every day from April to Oct, 11:00–18:00, in the former toll-booth on the Pont Louis-Philippe; b) Association sur les Chemins de Compostelle welcomes pilgrims in the cathedral 16:00–19:00, 13/4–20/9. Gîte d'Etape Le Relais des Jacobins, 12 Rue des Jacobins (near Pont Cabessut and Eglise du Sacré-Coeur, 05.65.21.00.84, 15pl, camping possible, K, but not for groups). Association pour l'habitat des Jeunes du Quercy, 129 Rue Fondue-Haute (05.65.35.29.32, open all year, phone ahead) also puts up walkers/pilgrims, K). Youth hostel in Foyer des Jeunes Travailleurs, 20 Rue Frédéric Suisse (near Mairie, 05.65.35.64.71, 45pl, open all year). 3 CH, 5 hotels. Camping Rivière de Cabessut, Rue Rivère, by river to NE of town, April–September.

Large town (population 21,000) surrounded on three sides by the river Lot. Important pilgrim halt and a good place for a rest day. Cathedral of Saint-Etienne with cloisters, several interesting churches and secular buildings. Pont Valentré (finest fortified bridge in Europe), museum. Ask in TO for a town plan with walking route.

After turning L under railway line turn R at traffic lights at end of **Rue du Barry** into the **Place de la Resistance** (at side of main road), go up steps (L), cross over main road and cross the river **Lot** by the **Pont Louis Philippe**.

At the Accueil Pèlerins in the former tollbooth on the LH side of the bridge you can have your pilgrim passport stamped, obtain information about accommodation and the route ahead and have a cold drink.

Then (the GR65 as such does not enter the town centre) you have a choice:

a) To visit Cahors: after crossing the bridge continue ahead along the **Boulevard Gambetta** to **Place Aristide Briand** *(Mairie, TO)*. To continue (and pick up the GR65) turn L shortly afterwards down **Rue Wilson** which leads you (crossing railway line via an underpass at the end of this street) to the **Pont Valentré**. *(If you look up before you cross you will see the Croix de Magne on the skyline to the L.)* Cross the bridge *(note 18th century wine-press to L)*.

b) To continue without visiting Cahors: after crossing the bridge turn L along the **Quai Eugène Cavaignac**, continue along the **Allées des Soupirs** and then turn L over the **Pont Valentré**.

Note sculpture of the devil on the upper RH side of the second tower. The story goes that when the bridge was first built, at the beginning of the 14th century, the master mason in charge of the work despaired of ever getting it finished in time. So he did a deal with the devil who, in exchange for the mason's soul, agreed to get the construction finished. However, when it was nearing completion, the mason, still hoping to save his soul, sent the devil off to a spring to fetch water for the building work – but in a sieve! Realising that he had been tricked the devil backed out, but in revenge removed a stone from the central tower and cast a spell on it so that every time it was replaced it would dislodge itself again. When the Pont Valentré was restored in 1879 the architect noticed that there was still a stone missing, and decided to fill the space with the sculpture of a devil clutching at the cornerstone he tries desparately, but always in vain, to extract.

Pick up waymarks on other side of the bridge where, once again, you have a choice:

a) 'Passage sportif' – the main GR65: turn *left* at end of the bridge, where a steep FP to your R, fitted with handholds to stop you slipping, zigzags its way uphill (watch out carefully for waymarks) and then levels out a little. It passes the top of a water treatment tower and then > a bigger track. Follow it until you reach a minor road at radio masts. *(Very good views of Cahors and the Pont Valentré as you climb.)*

However, although the steep section is not very long, if you have a large/heavy rucksack, if you are not very agile, if you don't like scrambling or if the weather is wet (and therefore slippery) you may prefer not to take the waymarked

Caselle near Cahors

'passage sportif' up the cliffs but take the 'déviation équestre', an alternative, way-marked in orange. This is 1km longer, missing out the **Croix de Magne**.

b) 'Déviation équestre' – turn *right* after crossing the bridge and immediately afterwards fork L down a road closed to traffic from this end, the **Route de Lacapelle** (uphill – *do NOT follow the red and white* balises *here, which are for the GR6, not 65*), veering L to join a road coming from back R. About 300m later, at bend, turn L up **Côte de la Croix de Magne (C1)**, zigzagging uphill. At crossroads at top turn L (**Chemin de la Croix de Magne**) to go to the cross or KSO on road to pick up GR65 waymarks (which come from your L).

1km Croix de Magne 223m (341/397)

A very large cross, visible from the town near the Pont Valentré.

Turn R and follow this road to crossroads *(bus stops to R)* and turn L ('déviation équestre' *joins the route here)*.

Turn L at T-junction 100m later (road bridge to R) and follow road down to N20, ignoring turnings. Go through the tunnel under the N20 at bottom of hill.

Veer L on other side and turn L (over tunnel) and KSO on this minor road (**Route de Fontanet** to begin with, becoming the **Route des Matthieux**), ignoring turns *(occasional shade, not too much traffic)* for 1.5km along the valley. KSO uphill to junction with iron wayside cross in hamlet of **Les Mathieux**. Fork R uphill on **Chemin de la Courounelle et des Mathieux**. About 150m later fork R onto FP uphill through woods, reach small tarred road and turn L. KSO. Continue on **Chemin du Pech de Gadal**. Reach another road opposite *Gîte de la Domaine des Mathieux* (gîte d'étape & CH, 05.65.31.75.13, 28pl, April–Oct, K).

Turn L here but then immediately R, downhill, on rough track. Turn L to better track, downhill, but less steeply, go under bridge and reach road (D653). Cross over and KSO on small FP on other side, lined with young trees. Cross wooden FB (dried-up stream) and turn R onto grassy track that > shady gravel lane. KSO(R) at fork and R again at next fork, almost immediately. Reach track coming from back R and turn L uphill.

Near the top fork R (LH turn is marked 'propriété privée'). KSO then, when track levels out a bit, turn hard L at junction uphill again.

When you reach the beginnings of a residential area KSO ahead on road and reach junction with the D7 at the entrance to village. Cross over and KSO ahead on other side *(picnic table)* up towards church in...

8km Labastide-Marnhac 257m (349.5/388.5)

Phone box, ♣ behind church. Camping à la ferme (April–August) near entrance to L.

*(To visit **Saint-Remy**, 30min, a pilgrim hospital built in 1286, turn R after church, a variante GR, waymarked. To return to GR65 either retrace your steps or take the D67.)*

To continue: KSO, pass church (L), Mairie (L), join D7 and KSO(L) along it. About 50m later fork L onto track (by *caselle* on L). At crossing of unsurfaced tracks 500m later KSO. *(Around 2km after Labastide-Marnhac turn L for* variante GR65 via **L'Hospitalet**, *1.5km away, with CH, campsite open all year.)*

KSO, ignore RH turn, KSO(L) at fork, passing isolated house on R (**Maison Gâteau**). KSO(R) at fork and reach T-junction of similar tracks. *All this stretch is fairly level.*

Turn L and 200m later reach minor road by farm (**Trigodina**) and turn R along it. At crossroads 500m later KSO, after which road > unsurfaced after large isolated house on RH side.

KSO on ridge *(this is the old Hospitalet–Lascabanes road)*. After 3km, still on ridge, turn hard L (when you least expect it) onto another track, veering R. KSO(L) at fork and reach minor road, at the inside of a U-bend. Cross over and fork L (not straight ahead) down track. Another track joins from back L at opening on plateau; KSO ahead. KSO ignoring turns.

When you reach another road *(iron wayside cross L, picnic area to R with covered seating)* cross over and KSO(L) ahead, diagonally, along track. KSO. When track begins to rise slightly fork R at junction to grassy track veering L and then R downhill into wide bowl-like valley. When green lane joins from R KSO(L) along it and downhill (> tarred) to minor road in hamlet of **Baffalie**. Turn R along it for 200m then turn L (by small wooden wayside cross) down grassy track along side of field, veering L at end by *lavoir*. Do *not* cross bridge (to D7) but KSO(L) ahead on very minor road and turn R at next crossing by large house in spacious grounds. Emerge on D7 by Mairie in…

11.5km Lascabanes 180m (361.5/376.5)

Gîte d'Etape Le Nid des Anges in former presbytery (adjoining church, 05.65.31.49.12 & 05.65.31.86.38, 17pl, phone ahead, open from 13h, open all year), CH 100m before village, by castle (05.65.22.92.63 & 06.73.07.46.37). Pilgrim blessing in church every evening at 18:00. ♣ by church. Lascabanes had a pilgrim hospital in the 15th century.

To continue either pass to RH side of Mairie, turning R and then R again or cross D7 and continue to church and *gîte,* then continue on minor road (marked 'St Géry/Sabatier') and 300m later (at bend) KSO ahead up unsurfaced road and then uphill into woods, along walled lane (note *gariotte* to R) until you reach a minor road (1km from Lascabanes). Turn R along it for 1km to junction with the **Chapelle Saint-Jean-le-Froid** on the LH side and then turn L.

The chapel is always open, a good place for rest/shelter. (Fête and Mass in Occitan last Sunday in June.)

Continue ahead past chapel, pass to R of farm *(♣ to L)* and veer R uphill on unsurfaced track. KSO. When you reach a road at a sharp RH bend turn hard L then immediately R onto track (in effect continuing in a straight line from where you have come from).

At junction of tracks on ridge in open heathland KSO ahead. Reach D37, turn L and then 20m later turn hard R onto gravel lane alongside field that winds its way past more fields and then over heathland on ridge. KSO(L) at fork 700–800m later. KSO at next and at fork *(seat, splendid views)* fork L. About 400m later reach D4, turn R along it and KSO.

For the variante *GR65 avoiding Montcuq – shorter, waymarked – take sec-ond L 500m later onto minor road marked 'Barnac' and then turn R immediately through fields. This rejoins the main GR65 1.5km south of Montcuq, just before the D28.*

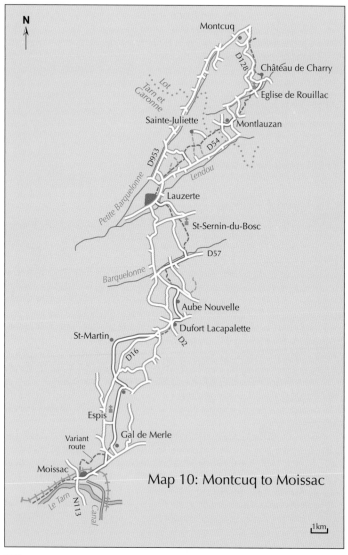

Map 10: Montcuq to Moissac

Otherwise, KSO(L) at fork then 200m later fork R onto minor road marked 'La Mothe 0,7', veering L, and continue on ridge. Road > unsurfaced after a while, descending gently at first *(FP to Gîte Le Souleillou on L, just before radio mast)* and then more steeply, veering L at end into **Place du Sol**, a square *(with ♣ and remains of another* métier à ferrer les boeufs) opposite a church in…

9km Montcuq (369.5/368.5)

Shops, cafés, several restaurants. Gîte d'Etape Le Souleillou, 22 Rue du Souleillou (05.65.22.48.95, 29pl, all year, camping possible, K). Camping municipal Saint-Jean (15/6–5/9) with tent available for pilgrims. TO (8 Rue de la Promenade). 2 hotels, 4 CH.

Small hilltop town dominated by 12th-century keep. Church of Saint-Hilaire and a second church. More or less the halfway point between Le Puy and Saint-Jean-Pied-de-Port.

To visit town: KSO past church to R up **Rue du Faubourg** and then retrace your steps to continue. *(Useful town plan on board at entry.)*

To continue: turn L along **Rue du Pontet** (D28), cross bridge and 50m later fork L uphill up tree-lined lane. Continue on ridge at top on open track through fields and at wide track turn R and then 80m later turn L along D28. Variante *rejoins main GR65 from L here (1.5km from Montcuq).*

About 150m later at RH bend KSO(L) down very minor road, descending gently and then turn R onto FP a few metres after road enters woods. Pass entrance gates to **Château de Charry** (L, *handy seat*) and KSO on FP through woods. Cross D28 (**Roux**, a farm, to L, and wayside cross – this is **Berty**) and KSO on other side, downhill down green lane. Turn R at bottom along minor road and then you can a) fork L uphill for 300m to visit church in **Rouillac** *(Romanesque frescoes on ceiling above altar)* and then retrace your steps, and/or b) KSO(L) ahead (marked 'Carros 0,6').

After about 1km turn L down unsurfaced track through fields, cross the **Tatuguié** (stream) by metal footbridge and continue ahead alongside fields, veering R, L and R again *(small lake to R)* uphill (slippery in wet weather) to road in hamlet of **Bonal** (1km).

Fork R along road *(Montlauzan ahead on hill)*. About 600m later KSO(L) at junction and continue on road *(another big lake to R)*. Turn R uphill at T-junction and KSO *(note topiary wayside cross to L),* ignoring turns to…

7km Montlauzan (376.5/361.5)

You are now in the *département* of the Tarn et Garonne. For gîte & CH in former presbytery, 200m off route, turn hard R at top of hill (05.65.36.04.02 & 06.73.44.26.39, 5pl, Easter to 1/11.)

The GR65 does not enter the village so do not turn hard R at top of hill but KSO downhill instead, on D256, to the D45. Turn L along it for 100m then turn R up path alongside vines at first, then continue on FP to L of hedge, uphill all the time into woods.

Topiary wayside cross at entry to Monlauzan

Emerge briefly onto open plateau *(more or less level with Montlauzan church behind you)* then re-enter (semi-shaded) woods. KSO, ignoring turns. After 2km reach minor road at bend and KSO(R) along it. KSO at junction (L turn to Al Casse, R to Sainte-Juliette) and then KSO(R) down unsurfaced track (at LH bend in road), alongside long wire fence. KSO for 1.5km on dead straight, shady FP until you reach a minor road at...

3.5km Le Pech-de-la-Rode (380/358)

Here you can either a) *(in bad weather)* turn L and then R on D45 and KSO to Lauzerte or b) continue on FP ahead *(very slippery and dangerous in wet weather)* and reach minor road at a farm (**Raissou**). Fork R down a shady lane here, following it round along side of fields, gently downhill, until you reach the D54 2km later. KSO(R) along it to a roundabout *(large superstore on R, café, tabac/presse to L)* and continue ahead on D2 uphill

Halfway up hill turn R up steep grassy lane. Turn R at top then immediately L up unsurfaced road *(gîte d'étape 'Les Figuiers' on R, 05.63.94.61.29 & 06.85.31.71.31, 38pl, all year, K),* hard L at top onto road. Turn R, veering L into **Place des Cornières** in the centre of...

3.5km Lauzerte 221m (383.5/354.5)

Shops, cafés, restaurants, hotel, TO (Place des Cornières), gîte d'étape communal, Rue du Millial (05.63.94.61.94, 17pl, Mar–October, ask in TO or café in Place des Cornières, K). Gîte d'Etape, Rue de la Gendarmerie (06.85.45.60.88, 4pl, Easter–September, walking pilgrims only). Gîte + CH, on GR65 (05.63.94.61.29 & 06.85.31.71.31, 38pl, all year, open after 13:30, K).

Bastide hill town dating from 12th century. Medieval houses, two churches (Saint-Barthélmy, with modern statue of St James as pilgrim inside, and Eglise des Carmes).

To leave: cross the **Place des Cornières**, KSO ahead on **Rue du Marché** then turn R down **Grande Rue/Rue de la Gendarmerie** past tower (L) and then turn L down steps (this is the **Impasse de la Brèche**) by **Maison de Retraite**. Cross road and go down small stone staircase, turn L on road and immediately hard R down slope. Cross minor road and KSO ahead alongside cemetery wall (on your RH side), veering L. Turn R and 60m later fork L off road down grassy track *(watch out carefully for waymarks)* leading to road. Turn L ('no entry') then continue on D953 for 200m before turning R down D81 (marked 'St Jean').

Half-timbered dovecote, Quercy

Cross three bridges (the 3rd is over **Le Lendou**, a small river) then turn second R uphill (marked 'Péries') and KSO(R) up tarred road which > green lane *(lake to R)*, leading uphill (at times steeply) through woods (2km). *(Handy seat with good view back to Lauzerte at top.)*

At road turn L for 300m to the (much-photographed) *'pigeonnier du Quercy,'* a dovecote *(opposite* **Le Chartron**, *a big house)*, and 50m later turn R downhill on gravel track to small church in valley bottom.

Church of Saint-Sernin-du-Bosc

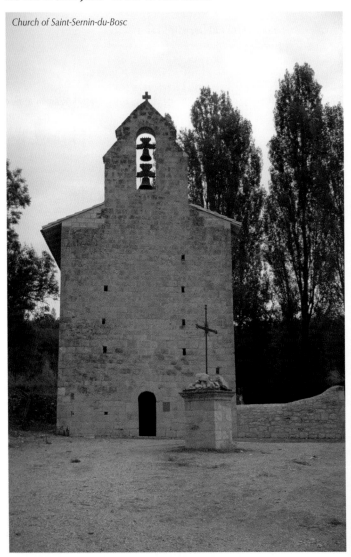

3km Eglise Saint-Sernin du Bosc (386.5/351.5)
Church of Romanesque origin, restored 1991 onwards.

KSO(R) uphill and 100m later turn R along minor road (*lake below to R*) and 200m later fork R along grassy lane along side of hill then fork R again at next fork, leading down to minor road near farm (**Parry**). KSO(R) veering L. At junction KSO ahead on another minor road and reach D57.

Turn R along it for 1.3km and then (after passing small crossroads and opposite track to R and 100m after crossing stream) turn L up wide grassy lane leading along side of woods. Follow line of trees, veering R uphill to minor road by house.

Turn L on minor road for 300m then continue ahead on road to top of hill. Turn L here (**Mirabel***)* then fork R 100m later before bending down lane between hedges *(old fountain to L)* leading downhill through fields.

Turn R, L and L again (round three sides of a square) and KSO ahead on grassy track which > shady lane, to valley bottom.

About 500m after turning L the 2nd time turn R over stream and continue uphill on muddy track veering L to farm. KSO(L) on minor road to…

5.5km Auberge de l'Aube-Nouvelle (392/346)
Hotel/restaurant (05.63.04.50.33).

At junction 100m later turn R steeply uphill to road *(but KSO ahead (to L) for the Gîte Le Pigeonnier de Figué-Haut, 05.63.04.56.32 & 06.70.89.88.05, 15pl, all year, camping possible – tents provided, K)*. Turn L along minor road just before you reach the D22, then fork R on grassy track alongside fields. Turn R again, veering R to D2 and continue on FP to LH side of road, up to a roundabout. KSO on D20 to a junction with bakery and bar/tabac alimentation in…

1.5km Dufort-Lacapalette 206m (393.5/344.5)
Bar/tabac/grocery store (X Wed), ♣ beside it, bakery (X Mon), post office.

Continue on D16 (towards Moissac) and after 1km turn R onto minor road to **Saint-Martin**, veering L. Turn L after 1.5km, passing church (to R), and descend to D16 again.

*However, unless you want to sleep in **Saint-Martin** (Gîte/CH, 05.63.04.41.58, 8pl, all year, K) or **La Baysse** (Gîte, 05.63.04.56.03, 5pl, all year) it is not worth the detour as the route is all on tarmac and there is hardly any shade either. Instead it is suggested that you stay on the D16 until you see the waymarks indicating a left turn onto a minor tarmac lane.*

Cross over and continue on small FP on LH side for 250m then turn L onto a minor tarred road, veering R, then at bend KSO(R) ahead on shady FP between hedges and fields. 1km later veer L, go up bank, turn R on minor road and 50m later return to the D16. Turn L onto FP below road and KSO.

Around 400–500m later turn L onto minor tarred road, veering R and continue on clear grassy track through fields, // to D16 most of the time. About 800m later turn L up FP leading uphill through trees to gravel lane coming from L; turn R along it (farm to L) and 400m later (at **Fournaise**) turn hard R along a minor road and KSO along it on ridge, passing farm at **Carbonières** (R), and continue to church (♣) and hamlet of…

9km Espis 152m (402.5/335.5)

Continue along ridge, ignoring RH turn before **Le Mole**, after which road begins to descend. KSO, going downhill to cluster of houses at…

3km Gal de Merle (405.5/332.5)

At junction at bottom of hill (HT pylons) KSO(R) ahead, cross footbridge over stream and 100m later reach D957 and turn L along it *(bench on L with shell on top, just before you reach the road, ♣).*

Turn L onto road (D957) just before town entrance boards and continue to a roundabout. Continue ahead here *(FP on RH side of road, ♣ at start).*

From here there is a *standard route* into Moissac and a *variante,* both waymarked.

a) For the standard route take the fifth turning R (opposite end of cemetery wall) into the **Chemin des Vignes**. This leads you, after some 1.5km, to the **Avenue du Chasselas**.

Turn R along it for 300m then fork R (just before tunnel under railway line) up **Chemin de Ricard** (to RH side of tracks) and 300m later turn L over level crossing. Continue ahead (**Côte de Landerose**) and then 100m later turn R. Go along **Faubourg Ste Blanche**, **Rue Général Gras**, **Rue Malaveille** and then turn R up **Rue de la République** to the abbey.

b) For the 'scenic route' (the *variante,* which has very good views, though you may not feel like it at the end of a long day) take the fourth R turn up the **Chemin de Malengane**. KSO for 1.5km and then turn L steeply uphill just before house no 643 *(waymark missing)* beside orchards for 150m to a minor road. Turn R and continue uphill again and onto a ridge, the **Croix de Lauzerte**. After 1km road begins to descend, KSO ahead at junction down the **Côte Saint-Michel**, descending steeply down grassy track *(plenty of seats)* and a tarred road to the old section of the town and the abbey.

2.5km Moissac 76m (408/330)

All facilities. Population 12,000 (twinned with Astorga, on the *Camino francés* in Spain). SNCF (trains to Agen, Bordeaux, Montauban, Toulouse). TO (6 Place Durand De Bredon). Accueil de la communauté réligieuse de Marie Mère de l'Eglise, 20 Boulevard Camille Delthil (phone ahead 10:00–12:00, 05.63.32.28.87, 7pl, Easter to 1/10, K). Gîte d'Etape in the Ancien Carmel, 5 Sente du Calvaire, high up on hill above the abbey (05.63.04.62.21 & 06.73.49.54.27, 66pl, all year, K). Gîte La Petite Lumière, 1183 Sente du Calvaire (below Ancien Carmel, 05.63.04.37.09 & 06.62.62.73.72, 6pl, April–Oct, K). Gîte d'Etape Ultreia + CH, 14 Avenue Pierre Chabrié (on GR opposite railway station, 05.63.05.15.06 & 06.71.74.03.14, 6pl, April–Oct K). Camping communal de l'Ile de Bidounet, 1km south of river (April–Sept). 3 CH, 4 hotels.

Major pilgrim halt from the Middle Ages onwards. Abbey church of Saint-Pierre, former Benedictine monastery founded in the 7th century with impressive cloisters; first built in 1100, they contain 116 columns and 76 capitals, 46 of which tell Bible stories or the lives of saints: a guided tour of the abbey is recommended. (Services: 08:30 Lauds, 12:15 Midday Prayers, 18:00 Vespers, all in abbey; 22:30 Compline, in priory.) Musée Saint-Jacques is in the former church (of St James). Centre d'Art Roman (Romanesque art) in former convent buildings to north of railway line near Abbey. Try to allocate at least half a day to visit the town.

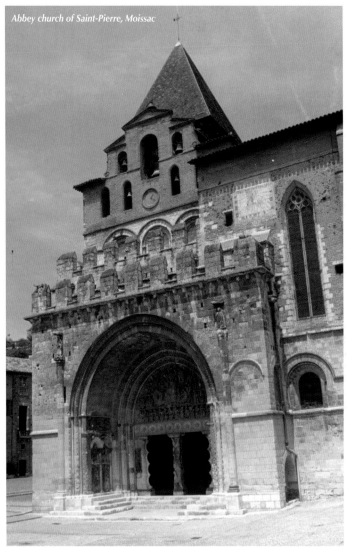

Abbey church of Saint-Pierre, Moissac

SECTION 3

Moissac to Aire-sur-l'Adour

To leave Moissac: from Abbey (facing the main entrance) turn L into the **Rue Marcassus/Carriera Sant Miquel** and turn L into **Allées de Marengo** (don't go up slope). Continue along **Avenue Pierre Cahabrie**, forking R up slope to railway station and then go down steps (L) ahead, cross **Avenue Gambetta** and then road bridge over the canal. Turn R along the **Promenade St Martin** on LH bank of canal. Continue along the canal towpath *(shady in parts)* to a lock.

3km Ecluse de l'Espagnette (411/327)

After that you have a choice:

a) The main GR65 *(not described here)* crosses the canal at the bridge and, presumably to vary the long, flat walk along the canal, goes up along a ridge, visible ahead of you, before coming down again in **Maulause**: strenuous but with good views over the 'lake' where the rivers **Tarn** and **Garonne** meet. The GR comes down briefly into **Boudou** *(village, shop, hotel-restaurant)* before climbing up again. After **Maulause** (9km) you continue along the towpath as in b) below.

b) The *variante* continues along the LH bank of the canal towpath and is the route described here. *However, neither this nor the main GR65 is the historic route: that crossed the Tarn in Moissac itself and continued south via St Nicholas de la Grave, thus missing out Auvillar, but the construction of the Autoroute des Deux Mers in the early 1990s necessitated considerable rerouting of the GR65. Both options are way-marked with the normal red and white balises. The towpath is fairly shady, particularly later on, quiet, in the main (especially after Maulause) and slightly shorter, and is suggested as a change after the constant ups and downs of the route until now and because there are no significant 'sights' on the higher level option anyway.*

Continue on the LH bank of the canal, pass a second lock 3.8km later (**Petitbezy**), go under the D26 road bridge *(picnic tables)* and pass a first brick bridge at **Ganneau**, at the beginning of Maulause, and then another bridge in...

7.5km Maulause 66m (418.5/319.5)

Gîte, Avenue de Bordeaux (05.63.39.64.23 & 06.79.44.09.77, 10pl, K), bar (X eve & Wed pm), shop (X Mon pm), bakery (X Mon) in village itself, bar/tabac. Picnic tables on RH bank by the second (concrete) bridge.

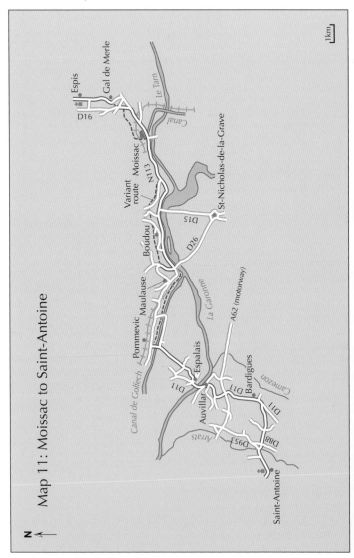

Map 11: Moissac to Saint-Antoine

At another similar bridge 1.5km later KSO ahead on LH bank. Pass a third lock and at the next bridge after that turn L over canal and continue on its RH bank for 400m to the **Pont de Pommevic** (a road bridge). *(About 100m before it, by seat, cross FB to village for shop, bar etc. and then retrace your steps.)*

3.5km Pommevic (422/316)

Hotel-Restaurant on RN 113, bar, shop (both X Tues & Sun pm), 12th-century church in village, accessible by FP to R shortly before you reach the bridge.

Go under bridge and turn R immediately up a FP and then hard R to cross the bridge over both canal and river.

Auvillar is visible on the hill ahead; campsite (Capelinos, open all year) on LH side of road after crossing bridge. KSO ahead (marked 'Espalais 3'), KSO at crossroads and veer R just before entry to village of…

3.5 Espalais 63m (425.5/312.5)

New gîte reported at 34 Avenue de Monplaisir.

Continue to end of village, pass church *(R, ♣, nice public garden with seats)* and turn L to cross road bridge (carefully) over the **Garonne.**

Turn L on other side on **Espanade du Port**, fork R, pass Romanesque **Chapelle Sainte-Cathérine du Port** *(R, closed at present but there are plans to restore it, ♣)* and zigzag steeply uphill on **Chemin du Peyret**. At large renovated *lavoir* (R) turn hard L uphill on **Rue de la Fontaine** then R, passing gîte d'étape (R) and enter the **Place de la Halle** in…

1.5km Auvillar 108m (427/311)

Shops, cafés, restaurants. Gîte d'étape communal (phone TO, 05.63.39.89.82, 18pl, all year, K) in former presbytery. 2 small private gîtes (all year), 6 CH, Hotel-Restaurant, TO (1 Place de la Halle) but no ATM.

Small town on hilltop with circular medieval market hall, very well restored, in arcaded square. Church of Saint-Pierre, museum.

Continue R ahead along **Rue de l'Horloge**, passing under arch, and KSO ahead uphill *(**Rue de la Sauvetat**, the D11 to Bardigues)*, veering R uphill. Turn L at top of hill, turn L onto minor road (marked 'Hautes Peyrières') just before town exit

Rue de l'Horloge, Auvillar

boards. Veer R at last house down grassy track leading downhill, then slightly up 500m later, to D11 again, by bridge over stream. Turn L, go under motorway and continue on D11 towards…

4km Bardigues (431/307)

Bar/restaurant by church (in village itself, to L of road), CH (05.63.39.60.30).

Continue on D11 for 350m then just before village exit boards turn R down minor road and continue on plateau for 1.5km to a T-junction. KSO *ahead* down unsurfaced track which > FP (overgrown to begin with) which leads in more or less a straight line downhill past farm (R, **Saint-Antoine** *visible to L ahead here*) and via a tarred road to D88 (1km). Cross over, marked 'Saint-Antoine 1,5', veer R and then turn L over bridge over the river **Arrats** and KSO on road (D953) for 1km to…

5km Saint-Antoine 73m (436/302)

Gîte d'Etape & CH (05.62.28.64.27, 30pl, to R of road on leaving), bar/restaurant/shop (7/7 April–Oct).

The village takes its name from the religious order of the Antonins, who set up a hospital (the present château) for people suffering from ergotism (a disease also known as 'St Anthony's fire'), which was very prevalent in the Middle Ages. It was contracted by consuming cereal products (such as rye bread) contaminated by the ergot fungus, and resulted in a gangrenous condition of the hands and feet. There was a similar such hospital further along the *Camino Francés*, the pilgrim road to Santiago in Spain, shortly before Castrojeriz.

The church has two murals discovered in 2006 (and due to be restored): a) St George and the dragon, 14th century and b) the story of St Blaise (who was martyred by being skinned alive), 16th century.

You are now in the *département* of the Gers, whose Conseil Général has made a strenuous effort to provide footpaths for pilgrim use alongside all its major roads used by the GR65 (until Aire sur-l'Adour, where you enter the département of Les Landes) and requests you to use them for both your own safety and that of other road-users.

Continue through village, veering L, go under arch onto pedestrianised street, passing bar/restaurant/shop. At crossing 1km later KSO ahead then, at top of hill, by farm, continue ahead but then, almost immediately, fork R down grassy track

Map 12: Saint-Antoine to Flamarens

ahead, downhill, down shady lane. Cross field, then stream, continue up on other side, pass farm, more or less in a straight line all the time, and KSO on minor road up to village of…

4.5km Flamarens 210m (440.5/297.5)

Accueil Chrétien des pèlerins (05.62.28.61.13 but only 48h ahead, 4–5pl, all year, donation). New CH on route itself by castle at 21 Au Village (05.62.28.59.86, all year). ♣ by Mairie. Castle (12th–15th century) is a historic monument, being restored, but can be visited during July and August (10:00–12:00 and 14:00–19:00, X Tues). Eglise Saint-Saturnin.

The undulating countryside in this area consists mainly of cornfields and hundreds of acres of sunflowers, all lined up like battalions of well-trained soldiers who turn their heads towards the sun en bloc, according to the time of day.

Château de Flamarens

Map 13: Flamarens to Marsolan

N ←

1km

Turn R at 'stop' sign (D953) and then immediately L to church by large wayside cross. Go down path to R of castle to road and KSO along it, past another wayside cross, for 750m. Just before top of hill turn L down minor road (marked 'Gauran, Le Casse, Maynard') then 150m later, by fork, fork R down FP which > grassy track downhill, between fields, veering R to minor road then KSO(L) on FP to its LH side. Around 1.5km later pass *lieu-dit* **Biran** (*on R, small gîte d'étape, 05.62.28.64.65, 7pl, camping, all year, K*) then junction with D28. KSO ahead uphill, veering L to pass plantation of trees (on R).

Reach minor road on a ridge, at a U-bend. Fork L and KSO, downhill on FP to side of road. Continue (L) along D953 (*the* **Route de Valence**; *Point d'Accueil and Info-Pèlerin at house on RH side*) to reach junction with D19 and turn L up it into…

4km Miradoux (444.5/293.5)

Bar/restaurant with rooms, 6 Route de Lectoure (05.62.28.61.43). Accueil pèlerin La Pause Verte, 17 Route de Valence (on R at entry to village, 05.62.28.66.57 & 06.74.65.89.58 but preference to pilgrims who do not reserve, 8pl, camping in field, donation.) 2 CH (3 Place de la Mairie, 05.62.28.84.35 & 06.75.57.49.29) + 16 Grande Rue (05.62.28.69.19). Bakery, superette, bank (+ATM), post office, pharmacy, TO in Mairie. ♣. Picnic area by Salle des Fêtes.

Gothic church (modern statue of St James pilgrim inside). Fontaine de Condé.

Veer R, pass church and leave village on D953 (**Route de Lectoure**). About 200m after junction of D953 (to 'St Clar') and D23 ('Lectoure 14'), 1km from Miradoux, at bend, turn 2nd L up minor road, marked 'Tucoula'. When this bends R 50m later KSO(L) ahead up grassy track and then turn R uphill. At three isolated chestnut trees on ridge turn L along grassy track coming from farm to R (*view of Château de Fieux over to R*) and passing above **Château de Gachepouy**.

KSO at junction of similar paths by **Ferme de Gachepouy** (to R). Turn R at end of field along similar track coming from L. KSO(L) ahead when similar track joins from back R and go downhill to reach the D23. Turn L, cross stream and continue on FP to LH side of D23 for 500m. At entrance to village, just before its place-name boards, turn L onto minor road then R onto street, cross a road and continue ahead (*Accueil Pèlerin partway up on R*) to **Place de l'Eglise** in…

5km Castet-Arrouy (449.5/288.5)

Gîte communal (Mairie 06.84.92.73.96 or Mr Sala 05.62.28.73.97 & 06.22.18.42.76, 18pl, Mar–Nov, camping possible, K), Restaurant 'La Plancha' opposite church, 2 CH (05.62.28.77.47 & run by former pilgrim, 05.62.29.19.40 & 06.82.00.29.15 but reservations only 2 days ahead or same day). Covered sitting area in church porch, with tables.

Village name means 'red castle', originally the site of a small fort. Church begun in Gothic times with later additions has statues and newly restored 19th-century paintings (free guided tours daily May–Sept, 10:00–12:00, 15:00–19:00).

To continue KSO through village past church. KSO(L) on FP to LH side of D23 then change to RH side of road. KSO then, at end of woods, change back to LH side and KSO. Pass electricity tower, KSO and 700–800m later past turning (R) to **Bidou**. About 100m later cross road and turn R uphill alongside fields, then through woods and KSO, following line of hedge.

Around 1km from leaving road pass turning (L, over FB) to **Ferme Barrachin** (gîte d'étape, CH, 05.62.68.84.57, 5pl, April–Oct, no groups, K, camping) and KSO ahead. Pass LH turning with bridge over stream by pond and KSO first to RH side of stream then to L. KSO; 1km later pass large rectangular pond (R) then turning to **Boué** (a farm, CH, 05.62.68.89.49) to R and KSO, gradually uphill, then 100m later, at crossing, turn R on grassy track, leading up into the woods. KSO and 1km after that reach lane by **Pitrac** (large house to R). Turn L uphill on very minor tarred road for 500m, leading to the N21.

Turn L along it for 50m then turn R down track (passing house on L with gîte d'étape, ask next door – this is the lieu-dit **Tarisson** (Gîte, 2nd house on L after N21, 05.62.68.92.73, 6pl, Mar–Oct, K). Continue on grassy track between fields (view of Lectoure to R ahead), descending gradually but 150m before a farm turn R along side of field. Reach minor road, turn R then veer L 30m later. Around 400m after that fork L down lane. Fork L down grassy track at next fork, between fields, veering R alongside hedge. Reach minor road 800m/1km later and turn L downhill. KSO then go uphill, passing cemetery (on R, handy seat). Turn R by very large red wayside cross (**La Croix Rouge**) then, veering L, turn L (♣ to L) then turn R (**Rue Corhaut**). Turn 2nd R up **Rue Saint-Gervais** to the cathedral in…

10km Lectoure 186m (459.5/278.5)

Population 4000. All facilities. Accueil pèlerin in cathedral porch, Tues & Fri, 16:00–18:00, June–Sept including Accueil Chrétien in presbytery (05,62.68.83.83, reservations 24h ahead max,10pl, 6/4–27/9, donation). Gîte'd'étape L'Etoile Occitane, 140 Rue Nationale (05.62.68.82.93 & 06.74.45.11.17, 14pl, April–Oct after 14:00, K). Gîte, Résidence du Marquist (05.62.68.71.27, all year, K). Gîte-CH Le Pèlerin d'Occident, 28 Rue Sainte-Claire (05.62.28.50.35 & 06.88.90.55.74, 9pl, all year, K). Gîte-CH run by former pilgrim, 32 Rue l'Abbé Tournier (05.62.68.49.58, & 06.32.02.81.64, all year). 3 CH, 2 hotel-restaurants, TO (Place du Général de Gaulle).

One of the oldest towns in the Gers. Cathedral of SS Gervais & Protais, 17th–18th-century Hôtel de Ville, ramparts, many interesting old houses (Lectoure is also a spa town). Ask in TO for walking tour leaflet.

To continue, pass to RH side of TO (**Rue Fontelie**), veering L and then R downhill, down flight of steps, veering L past ramparts. Turn R onto **Chemin Claude Ydron** to junction of D7 and N21, turn L and 40m later go down minor road, the **Chemin de la Tride** (wedged between the N21 and the D7, to R), downhill. Turn R at bottom along D36 for 100m then turn L, go over level crossing and immediately turn R for 500m along minor road // to railway line. Just before *second* level crossing (to R) turn L onto D7. Cross the **Pont de Pile** over the river **Gers** and 100m later, before another bridge, turn hard R, veering L along wide grassy lane between hedges (semi-shaded).

Fork L at junction with similar track, reach the D36, cross it and KSO on minor road on other side. KSO(L) at junction and KSO, continuing on grassy track through fields after tarred surface ends at a farm (not well waymarked in 2009).

Halfway up hill pass to other side of hedge and KSO. Just before farm *(over to R ahead)* turn L onto unsurfaced road, veer L 100m later up to road *(good views back to Lectoure as you climb)* in hamlet of…

4.5km Espasot 160m (464/274)

Turn R *(useful stone seat 50m later)* and KSO for 2.5km along ridge *(very little shade)*. About 100m after a crossroads *(camping and CH Le Nauton Saint-Jacques signposted to R here)* with a stone cross *(a* croix de justice, *picnic area with information board)* fork R down grassy lane. Track joins from back R, KSO. Pass

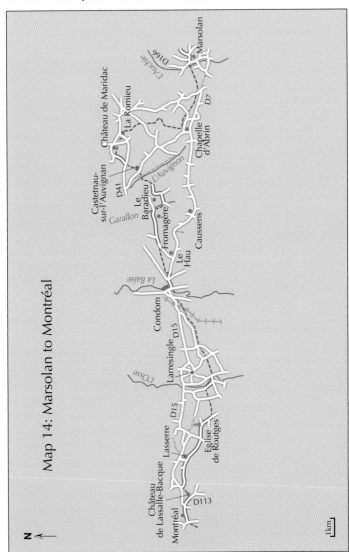

Map 14: Marsolan to Montréal

another small stone cross on pedestal (R) and KSO. Cross track, KSO. After 1km reach tarred road at junction and turn L, passing cemetery in…

4.5km Marsolan 171m (468.5/269.5)

Gîte/CH (05.62.68.79.40, all year X July/Aug) Remains of Hôpital Saint-Jacques at entrance to village. Shady square behind church good place to rest (♣ nearby). Covered rest area. Phone box.

Enter by Mairie and large wayside cross, pass to R of church and continue down-hill to cross D166. Continue on other side, KSO at crossing 200m later then turn L, veering R at bend onto grassy track leading up through fields. Pass small lake (L) and continue up to minor road at bend (2.5km). KSO(R) along it, KSO(L) at junction and when tarmac stops at last house KSO along grassy track along ridge *(good views)* before descending to continue ahead (in more or less a straight line all the time) through fields. KSO. Join minor road coming from back R just before a farm (**Bertsuguières**), pass farm of **Montravail** and turn R down track (downhill), 100m before you reach the Chapelle d'Abrin.

Chapelle d'Abrin

However, if you want to go directly to Condom, missing out La Romieu (6km shorter), you can KSO ahead here for 4km, to the RH side of the river Auvignon, rejoining the GR65 500m after it leaves Castelnau-sur-l'Auvignon, where you turn L onto it. For a description of this option see page 141.*

5km Chapelle d'Abrin (473.5/264.5)

Former commandery of the Knights Hospitallers of St John of Jerusalem (now a private house), pilgrim halt at meeting of two routes (the other came from Rocamadour and Moissac via Agen).

Pass lake (R), KSO(R) uphill at fork and KSO. After 800m at top of hill (track bends L) KSO ahead downhill along green lane, through fields and uphill into woods. Turn L at top of hill at T-junction, leave woods, reach road at bend and turn R for 80m. Turn L along track. Opposite farm (**Le Double**) turn hard R alongside woods onto another track and descend gently to La Romieu, veering R at entry, then turn L at T-junction and immediately R along the **Rue Surmain** (to visit town) or L along D41 to continue. Gîte de Moncade, 500m off GR, 1km before La Romieu (05.62.28.84.61 & 06.71.58.50.21, 35pl, all year (but only for groups of at least 6) K).

5km La Romieu (478.5/259.5)

Gîte d'étape privé Le Couvent de La Romieu, in former convent, next to church (05.62.28.73.59, 15pl, 15/3–Oct, K, also rooms). CH, 2 Rue du Docteur Lucante (05.62.28.60.67). CH & Café-restaurant d'Angeline, Place Bouet (05.62.28.10.29. & 06.69.63.88.99). Camping-Restaurant Camp de Florence (May–Sept). Shop, bakery, TO (Rue du Docteur Lucante).

The village takes its name from the *romieux* (pilgrims) who passed through it on their way to Santiago. Like Condom and Lectoure, La Romieu also has an enormous church for its size, an indication of its former importance; the 14th-century Collégiale (built by Clement V, one of the Avignon Popes) is well worth a visit.

To leave: turn L on D41 then turn R down grassy lane (150m after *road* turns to R) through fields. Turn R at bottom (on minor road) and 150m later turn L towards **Château de Maridac** and veer R alongside it 300m later down green lane and KSO to road. Turn L (ignoring first RH turn) uphill. Turn L at top and immediately R down unsurfaced track, veer L before farm and then KSO(L) downhill on grassy track to valley bottom. Cross the **Ruisseau d'Auvignon** and continue uphill ahead to road *(school to R, stone wayside cross)* at entrance to the village of...

5km Castelnau-sur-l'Auvignon (483.5/254.5)

Gîte des Arroucasses, CH + Accueil pèlerin in village itself (05.62.28.12.24, 12pl, all year, K).

In this part of France (as in Castillian Spain), you can often see quite far ahead to where you are going next, as the landscape is very open.

Cross over and fork L downhill (continue line of path you were already on) down shady lane, then 200m later *turn* R and then *fork* R down green lane. Cut through minor road at 'S' bend and KSO over bridge over river **Auvignon** *(variante joins from L here, just before bridge.).*

* Variante omitting La Romieu: *this is also waymarked with the normal red and white balises but only adequately so. However, it is easy enough to follow.*

KSO ahead past the **Chapelle d'Abrin** *(now a private house)* on minor road then 300m later, at bend, KSO(L) ahead on earth track through fields. About 300m after that, just before a junction with a gravel track thet veers L, turn L (at right angles) downhill on grassy track. Turn R 100m later then fork L 50m after that, veering L downhill *(farm over to R)* through fields and then R to minor road at bend. Turn R along it. Around 300m later KSO(L) ahead on unsurfaced road. Continue ahead in valley, with river **Auvignon** // over to your L, passing **Touquet** *(farm)* and then the entrance to **La Maurague** *(farm)* to L. Some 4km after the **Chapelle d'Abrin** turn L, cross bridge over the river and rejoin the main GR65 coming downhill from your R.

After crossing the bridge continue ahead along green lane, fork L at junction and KSO to top of hill, passing to L of farm (**La Baraille**) and veering R on road to...

1.5km Chapelle Sainte-Germaine de Soldanum 168m (485/253)

Chapel from 12th–13th century, all that remains of former monastery (destroyed in 9th century by the Normans), dedicated to a local saint. The church, now partially restored, is normally open when the cemetery is. ♣ behind gate. Good (shady) place for a rest.

Continue on road to hamlet of **Baradieu**, turn L by pond and 400m later turn R by isolated barn down unsurfaced road to **Moras** (restored farm). Pass to R of it (lake to R), veer L, cross stream (stepping stones) and then turn R immediately along hedge and KSO alongside lake (**Bousquetara**). Veer L uphill onto tarmac lane, pass (on L) farm of **La Fromagère** and 1km later, at top of hill, cross D204 and continue downhill, first on road, then on gravel lane, then on grassy track alongside field, descending, after 2km, to the junction with the GRP just before you reach the D7 (over to your R, at a house called **Bagatelle**).

Turn L down shady lane, continuing as a minor road to junction with the D7 (**Avenue Rhin et Danube)** on the outskirts of Condom. Turn R over the river **Baïse** and continue R along the D7 (**Avenue Rhin et Danube**, becoming the **Avenue du Maréchal Joffre**) and then turn L (**Avenue des Anciens Combattants**) to war memorial. *(Turn R here to **Rue Gambetta** for shops, post office, cathedral etc.)* Pass to RH side of it up **Rue Jean-Jaures** *(passing gîte d'étape in Centre Salvandy, R)* to **Place de la Liberté**. Continue along **Rue Buzon**, turn R onto **Quai Buzon** and either turn R here into **Rue Roques** for centre of town or turn L over **Pont des Carmes** to continue.

9.5km Condom 81m (494.5/243.5)

Population 8000. All facilities, gîte communal in Centre Salvandry, 20 Rue Jean Jaures (Mme Adoue, 05.62.28.23.80, 20pl, all year, K). Gîte de Gabarre, on towpath on River Baïse, 200m off GR and 1km to south of town centre (06.86.41.58.39, 40pl, 15/4–31/10, K). Gîte privé La Maison du Pèlerin, 10 Avenue des Anciens d'AFN (05.62.28.10.04 & 06.88.96.66.37, 10pl, all year after 13:00, RE, K). Gîte, 25 Avenue du Général de Gaulle (05.62.28.17.35 & 06.68.60.06.71, all year, K). CH (05.62.28.30.26). Four hotels. Camping municipal la Gauge (June–August).18(!) restaurants. TO (Place Bossuet).

Typical Gascon town situated on a spur between the rivers Gèle and Baïse, centre of the Armagnac industry. Cathedral of Saint-Pierre, churches of Saint-Bathélemey de Pradeau, Saint-Jacques and Saint-Michel. Musée de l'Armagnac, cloisters (now the Mairie).

Turn L immediately after crossing bridge *(the building on L at end, now a theatre, was formerly a Carmelite convent)* along upper (RH) of two FPs alongside river, the **Chemin de la Digue**. This passes behind the **Eglise Saint-Jacques**, *which originally had a hospital attached to it.*

The statue above the blocked-up doorway on the street side is not St James but St Joseph, a dedication made in recognition of the latter's help in alleviating the sufferings of plague victims in that quarter of the town, La Bouguerie.

KSO past the **church of Saint-Jacques** then veer R *(Gîte Zabarre 100m to L)* to the D931, cross it, continue on banked-up lane and then turn first L down a minor road at the fork with the D15 *(the* Chemin des Capots de Teste, *the area in which there was a second Hôpital Saint-Jacques, as well as two other non-St James hospitals plus leprosaria)*. The minor road takes you through a residential area. Turn R at end by roundabout and then turn L 100m later on minor road to the hamlet of **Ciprionis**.

At top of hill KSO at first junction and KSO(L) at second. KSO, passing **L'Inquiétitude** (a farm). *The linguistically-minded walker/pilgrim will already have noticed the place names 'Montravail' and 'Monrepos' elsewhere, with 'Monplaisir' still to come...*

Continue, passing other farms, for 2km, ignoring turns, and much more up than down. At sharp RH bend in road KSO(R) at fork near top of (present) hill; KSO(L) ahead along green lane, uphill to plateau. Unsurfaced road joins from R. KSO *(view of Larresingle to R ahead)* and 200m later reach road in a *lieu-dit* known as **Le Carbon**.

5km Le Carbon 179m (499.5/238.5)

To visit **Larresingle**, *a tiny fortified town, completely walled (restaurant, TO May–Sept, ♣ by cemetery), turn R along road at Le Carbon. This was the fortress of the Bishops of Condom in the Middle Ages and is well worth the 15min detour (in each direction) to visit. To return, however, you need not retrace your steps again but, via a minor road to the SW, you can pick up the GR65 where it crosses the D278, just before the Pont d'Artigues, turning R to cross it.*

If you prefer not to visit Larresingle, KSO ahead down green lane, downhill for 1km. At crossing with another track veer L and then R to skirt small pond and veer L down FP through woods (in effect continuing in a straight line from where you broke off). KSO to reach a road (D278), cross it and 200m later cross the…

3km Pont d'Artigues (502.5/235.5)

Originally a Roman bridge over the Osse, with five arches. In the Middle Ages there was a pilgrim hospital belonging, successively, to the Diocese of Santiago, the Knights of the order of Santiago and then the order of Saint Jacques-de-la-Foi-et-de-la-Paix, but there is no trace left of it today. There was also a church of Notre-Dame by the pilgrim bridge but nothing remains of this today either.

Pont d'Artigues

KSO to crossroads and turn R for 600m then turn L by HT pylon up grassy lane alongside trees (to your R) uphill into the woods. Cross minor road and KSO on gravel road which > a grassy track. Around Ikm later reach a minor road and turn R and then L at T-junction 500m later (at RH turn to hamlet of Routges).

2.5km Eglise de Routges (505/233)

About 100m ahead of you, off road, is the oldest church in the region (♿). Note the small door on the side of the church; this was the entrance used by the Cagots, an outcast population of uncertain ethnic origin. They were found mainly in this part of France and lived segregated lives until the end of the 19th century. Like many other pariah communities they were believed to be leprous, syphilitic, unclean and bearers of all types of evil. As a result they were only allowed to enter churches by a special side door reserved for their use and were not permitted to be buried in the cemeteries used by the rest of the population.

KSO ahead along ridge at staggered crossroads (D254) and KSO for 1km more, 300m after passing hamlet of **Laserre-le-Haut** *(gîte/CH, 05.62.29.57.98, 10 + 12pl, K).* KSO(L) at fork to **Le Glesia** *(former Gallo-Roman site)* and 200m later KSO(L) down green lane. About 1km later, at **Pages**, track > tarred, and 200m later at bend

Eglise de Routges, Cagot door

Map 15: Montréal to Manciet

(fountain) KSO ahead up green lane under trees, veering L. Just 1km later pass **Château de Lasalle-Baqué** and KSO(R) along D113. Turn L at junction with wayside cross (D15) then immediately R along D113 again (now **Rue Aurensan**) into…

6.5km Montréal-du-Gers 135m (511.5/226.5)

Gîte/CH/restaurant Le Relais Saint-Jacques, by bridge (05.62.29.43.07, 6pl, all year). Gîte Compostela at 10 Rue du 14 Juillet, near town centre (05.62.28.67.36 & 06.44.31.82.82, 14pl, 1 April to 31 October, meals available); CH, 15 Rue Aurenson (05.62.29.41.44, April–15/11, K). Shop, bakery, café, restaurants, TO (Place de l'Hôtel del Ville), ♣ by fountain.

Small town (population 1200) with 13th-century bastide, arcaded market place, 13th-century church, several interesting old houses, museum, ramparts. Galloroman villa at **Séviac** (2km, on variant route, worth visiting) also has gîte d'étape communal (05.62.29.48.57, 14pl, March–November) and CH (05.62.29.44.12) near site and Halte de la Ferme du Soleil (gîte/CH, 05.62.29.45.77 & 06.14.44.60.64).

Enter town down **Rue Aurensan**, turn L into square. Go down RH side of church (under arch) and then turn R along **Boulevard des Remparts**, veering R *(shady seats)* and then turn hard L downhill, hard R immediately to the D15 and hard L onto a shady minor road. Road gradually > an unsurfaced track. KSO. At turning (L) to **Sallepissan** KSO(R) ahead. About 1km later reach minor road at bend and turn L along it, uphill KSO(R) and KSO, ignoring turns, for 800m to a road. Turn L along it then, at farm (**Ribère de Bas**), fork R down track (marked 'Barrière de Ribère'). KSO(L) for 1km along the bed of an old railway line *(shady)*, cross metal bridge (**Château de Montaut** *to L*) over a track and then ahead L 30m later and L again under bridge (in order to do a 'right turn'). KSO along track for a few hundred metres, then veer L uphill to road. Turn L and 100m later turn R up track leading between vines, continuously along line of trees to L. Veer L to gravel lane coming from L, KSO along it and 100m later turn L through more vines. Continue on road after 200m by farm and 150m later KSO ahead along grassy track following line of telegraph poles alongside vines (to R).

Pass farm (L) at road coming from R, KSO ahead along a track, then veer R alongside woods (L) at minor junction. KSO for 600m to road (D29). Cross over, continue alongside vines (L) for 200m, cross road leading to farm (**Bédat**) and continue alongside more vines to the D31.

Cross the D31 and KSO ahead (slightly staggered to L) on minor tarred road. About 400m later turn L alongside vines, continue on FP and then on green lane *(tower visible ahead)* to cemetery (♣) in village of…

9km Lamothe 167m (520.5/217.5)

Gîte d'Etape/CH Le Repos des Pèlerins, opposite cemetery (05.62.09.40.65, 10pl, 1/3–15/11, K). ♣ in cemetery. 13th-century guard tower.

From Lamothe to Nogaro the walking is fairly flat and easy, if not all that interesting.

Turn L and then hard R downhill past church *(shady porch)* to valley bottom and turn L along former railway line (tracks removed). KSO for 7km, mainly shaded, very slightly uphill all the time.

Centre d'herbergement vacances after 4km, on GR itself, at Escoubet (05.62.09.93.03, April–October).

Pass turning (on R) to Camping-Restaurant Moulin du Pouy, 1km before entrance to town. Continue until you reach the D931 at the entrance to *Eauze (huge factory to R)*, turning R into the town by a large superstore. KSO into the **Place d'Armagnac** and church in the centre of…

7km Eauze 142m (527.5/210.5)

Population 4300. Shops, cafés, several restaurants. Accueil Pèlerins Béthanie, 34 Avenue de Sauboires (600m after church, 06.75.83.75.00 but no reservations X evening before, 8pl, all year – phone ahead in winter, evening prayers, donation). Gîte d'Etape (pilgrims only) 2 Rue Félix Soules, opposite TO (05.62.09.85.62, 23pl, all year, K). Hôtel-Restaurant Le Triana (05.62.09.99.21).

Former Gallo-Roman capital *(Elusa)* and Roman colony. Benedictine priory founded in 10th century and attached to Order of Cluny. Church of Saint-Luperc (a local saint) built by the Benedictines, finished 1521, using rubble and stone from Roman sites mixed with local brick. Contains two 17th century confessionals and, in side chapel, statue of St Roch pilgrim. Icons on long centre panel behind altar are modern (1977), by Nicholaï Greschny (Tarn artist). Numerous old houses, including Maison de Jeanne d'Albret, Museum (with treasury of 28,000 Roman coins) and Andalusian-style bullring (Arènes Nimeño II).

To leave, with church on your R turn L into **Rue Robert Daury** (pedestrianised) and go ahead down **Avenue des Pyrénées** (D931) for 500m then turn R down minor road by house no 58. Turn L at end and then continue up grassy track. Reach major road 500m later, cross over and continue on other side, past vines, cross minor road and KSO ahead. At junction of similar tracks turn R. Reach a minor road and turn L. About 300m later, at junction, KSO(R) ahead (marked 'Pennebert'). At RH bend in road by farm KSO ahead down gravel lane, KSO(R) at fork by goose farm and continue downhill. Turn R and then L alongside edge of large field, turn R at bottom corner along edge of two more fields *(stream below to R in trees)*, veering R at end and then turn L to cross FB over the **Bergou** (stream).

KSO ahead up RH side of next field, passing to other (RH) side of hedge halfway up and continue up old sunken tree-lined lane. Cross track, cross minor tarred road 1km later, KSO ahead along grassy lane, veer R up side of field and at T-junction of tracks turn L in front of vines to road 100m later.

Turn R *(first view of the Pyrenees on a clear day)*, pass farm (**Riguet**) and 400m later turn L *(opposite end of a line of woods // to road on other side)* between vines. Veer R downhill (hedge to L), cross stream (seasonal) and veer L and R then continue on sunken green lane to junction at top of hill.

7km Ferme de Peyret 160m (534.5/203.5)

For gîte d'étape associatif *in old school in* **Sauboires**, *800m further (05.62.03.73.98, 10pl, all year, K)*, turn R here and also for CH at La Hargue (05.62.08.50.05). Otherwise, to continue, KSO along green lane. KSO(R) on track coming from back L and go downhill between vines. Pass several lakes (a fish farm) to L and turn L onto the D122 past **Au Moulin du Puoy** (L) and KSO for 2km to…

4km Manciet (538.5/199.5)

Shop (X Mon). Hôtel-restaurant des Sports Chez Monique, Rue Principale (05.62.08.56.40).

Rural bullring for *courses landaises* (cattle races, held on the 2nd Sunday in September every year along with the village *fêtes*) on L at entry to village. La Bonne Auberge is on site of former commandery (with Hôpital Saint-Jacques and chapel) set up by the Spanish order of the Knights of Santiago. Church of Notre-Dame de la Pitíe has 'viewing kiosk' and prayer desk accessible from the street when church is closed.

After the level crossing the GR65 waymarks lead you R *(picnic area)* to continue on the **Rue des Ecoles** then turn L over FB to cross the D931 to the church on the other side. Turn R here, down the **Rue Centrale** *(shops)* and rejoin the D931 300m later at a 'stop' sign, continuing ahead (L) along it.

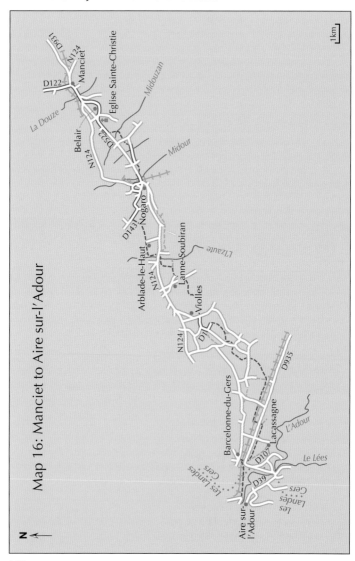

Map 16: Manciet to Aire sur-l'Adour

After 1km *(opposite former Manciet railway station, now a used-car dealership)* turn L along D153 (to 'Cravencères'). About 700m later (just before bend) turn R up unsurfaced road for 1km, passing farm **Bel Air** and then turn R 150m later onto tarred road. Turn L 200m later *(signposted also for the gîte d'etape Le Relais du Haget, 05.62.08.54.02 & 06.11.66.13.98, 10pl, 15/3–31/10, K)* by pond marked 'Tucon' and then R, marked 'Eglise Chapelle de l'Hospitalet'...

4km Eglise-hôpital Sainte-Christie (542.5/195.5)

This is the church of Saint-Jean-Baptiste de la Commanderie de Saint-Christie de l'Armagnac, formerly belonging to the Order of the Knights of Malta. The key to the church is normally available to allow visitors to make an inside visit but the building is kept locked at present as it is in a dangerous condition.

To continue, KSO ahead past cemetery and 50m later turn R (by an 18th century milestone with a Maltese Cross), following FP uphill and then into woods. At end KSO(R) along top side of field, with hedge to R and vines to L, veering L down towards road. Do NOT turn R here but KSO ahead, downhill on grassy track, // to the road. At junction turn 2nd L, passing to RH side of farm, and KSO ahead on gravel road, downhill to stream (**Saint-Aubin**).

Cross over (small FB) then turn R on other side, veering L, then alongside stream. Turn L uphill, forking R near to modern bungalow on minor road. Turn L, veering L, then 150m later turn R at earth track through fields, veering L. KSO down short lane, downhill to bend in minor road. Turn R downhill and 1km later reach crossing with discoidal cross. KSO ahead. Go down grassy bank after last house then down shady lane *(seats)*. Reach (tree-lined) D522 and 400m later enter...

5km Nogaro 98m (547.5/190.5)

Population 2000. All facilities. Gîte d'etape associatif (on GR leaving town, 05.62.69.06.15, 16pl, April–October, K), campsite (next to gîte, June–Sept). CH a) 8 Avenue du Midour (05.62.09.08.95 & 06.87.46.06.43); b) 17 Cité Nolibo (05.62.09.13.74 & 06.03.57.10.43), 2 hotels, TO (77 Rue Nationale).

Small town taking its name from '*Nogarium*' (a 'place planted with walnuts') and established in the 11th century. Romanesque church with former Hôpital Saint-Jacques nearby. Bullring.

Enter the town on the D522 (**Avenue de Midour**), go over level crossing then either turn R onto the D931 (**Avenue de Daniate**) for gîte d'étape or KSO ahead to continue.

At junction KSO ahead on **Rue Nationale** to church. At junction, fork R (D143) on **Rue Broque**, which then > **Avenue du Cassou de Herre**. KSO, continue uphill, past *château d'eau* (water tower) and KSO. Around 200m later the D143 veers R. Continue ahead here but at 2nd water tower you have a choice:

a) Main GR65: fork R onto a stony track which > earth track and KSO for 2km, downhill through woods, cross the **Jurone** (stream) and road > a track. Continue to **Claverie** (a farm) on road. Turn R then veer L downhill for 1km and L along stream, until you reach the D931 again. Turn R and cross the **Pont sur l'Izaute**…

b) Variante (slightly shorter): KSO(L) ahead on road *(not normally a lot of traffic)*, passing pond (L) and wayside cross, marked 'Arblade-le-Haut' and KSO. KSO(R) at fork 80m later then KSO for 3km (passing *Gîte/CH 'L'Arbladoise' on L 1.5km later, 05.62.09.14.11 & 06.14.75.90.24, 7pl, April–October X July, K*). Reach junction with D931 by the…

5km Pont sur l'Izaute (552.5/185.5)

In the section between Nogaro and Aire-sur-l'Adour there is a lot of road walking, but with very little traffic apart from tractors.

KSO on D931 for 600m then turn L down tree-lined lane. KSO for 2km to farm. *(Note buildings with* colombages, *Tudor-style woodwork typical of the Landes region and already encountered elsewhere.)* Pass between buildings *(Gîte/CH 'Maison Labarbe' to L, 05.62.08.83.81 & 06.63.33.87.49, 10–12pl, April–Nov after 15:00, K)* and continue (now a road) for 500m to D152 in the hamlet of…

3km Lanne-Soubiran (555.5/182.5)

Church on R has large porch – good place for shady rest.

Turn R for 500m along D152 and then turn L 250m later down minor road at small crossroads by village place-name boards, veering R. About 500m later KSO(L) along minor road coming from back R. Pass lake, veer R alongside woods and at sharp LH bend turn R along earth track through fields, veering L into woods, downhill. At T-junction of similar tracks at bottom turn L towards field but then, just before the edge of the wood, turn hard R along grassy lane. KSO, then KSO(R) at fork. Veer R and then L along edge of wood and continue through fields to road (1.5km). Turn L and then R 100m later up (more) minor road. Pass one farm and, just before a second, turn L downhill on minor road and then L 500m later turn L again at crossroads. This is **Ferme Castin** *(seat)*.

Veer R at fork 100m later and then 20m after that turn R down grassy track, veering L and then R slightly downhill and through fields. KSO. At crossing of tracks *(Ferme Dubarry over to L has gîte: 05.62.69.64.82 & 06.27.35.84.13, 12pl,1/4–15/11, K)* KSO(R) ahead R alongside vines (to R).

Pass alongside RH side of woods (vines to RH side now) and then turn L to enter woods. About 100m later reach minor road, turn R and 400m later reach minor road by church in village of...

7.5km Lelin Lapujolle (563/175)

Veer L by Mairie and reach D169 opposite a wayside cross and turn R. Around 150m later turn L up minor road, uphill, then L again 250m after that. At next crossing by houses, 750m later, turn R and 1200m later turn L up more minor road.

KSO for 1km then, 200m before you reach the D935, turn R on grassy track beside railway line and KSO. After 1.5km cross minor road and KSO again. About 800m later, by house, turn L over level crossing, veering R and then L and 300m later reach the D931. Cross over carefully *(there is a lot of very fast, heavy traffic)*. Continue ahead on other side. Road > gravel track, and then 200m later turn R between fields and KSO for 2km, // to main road over to your R.

Track > tarmac then fork R. Cross another road *(large superstore and super-market to R)* and KSO ahead on other side in....

17km Barcelonne-du-Gers (580/158)

Hotel-Restaurant Chez Alain, 6 Boulevard du Midi (05.62.09.44.39 & 06.81.27.57.47). CH/Accueil Pèlerins El Caracol run by two former pilgrims, 3 Route de l'Arblade (05.62.09.17.52, all year). Bakeries, another bar/restaurant.

At junction with very large restored *lavoir* KSO ahead. At crossing KSO ahead between houses on **Rue de l'Abattoir**, turn R at end into **Rue de Casamont** and then turn L into **Rue de l'Hôpital**. Join minor road coming from back R then turn L into **Chemin de Berret** then turn 1st R (**Chemin des Moncaux**) into **Chemin de Saligats**. Turn R at end then turn L by petrol station and large superstore *(with cafeteria)* onto the D931. KSO (pavement) and 800m later reach the D834. Turn L, cross the bridge over the river **Adour** and enter...

3km Aire-sur-l'Adour 81m (583/155)

Population 6200, all facilities. SNCF (buses). Accueil Pèlerins Paroisse Sainte-Quitterie, Cathédrale St-Jean-Baptiste & Presbytère every afternoon 14:30–18:30, April–October. La Maison des Pèlerin(e)s, 4 Rue Géneral Labat, run by former pilgrim (05.58.71.68.07 & 06.81.17.70.05, 12–14pl, April–Oct, K). Gîte d'étape privé Hospitalet Saint-Jacques, 21 Rue Félix Despagnet, on GR, also run by former pilgrims (05.58.03.26.22, 14pl, March–October, K, walking pilgrims only ie no back-up vehicles or baggage transfer service). Gîte d'étape in Centre de Loisirs on way out of town towards the Pont sur l'Adour (05.58.71.61.63, 60pl, all year X Fri & Sat nights, public holidays and previous evening, K, meals available). Hôtel de la Paix-Gîte, 7 Rue Carnot (05.58.71.60.70 & 06.81.38.50.02) has a special (cheap) pilgrim price including breakfast and gîte, 8pl, all year X 15 days in February, K). CH 17 Rue du Château (05.58.71.91.26 & 06.03.92.51.63). 3 other hotels. Campsite by river near bridge (Les Ombrages de l'Adour, 05.58.71.64.70 & 05.58.71.75.10, May–September, also rents caravans per person per night). TO (Place du 19 Mars 1962).

Ancient town in two parts: the lower section by the river with the cathedral of Saint-Jean Baptiste (12th-century but altered several times; AP 15:00–18:00 daily, pilgrim mass normally at 1:00), Mairie, and 19th-century Halle aux Grains; and the 'Mas d'Aire' or higher town with the brick-built Eglise de Sainte Quitterie built on site of Benedictine monastery.

Please note that since this edition was prepared it appears that there have been some waymarking changes in short sections of the route depicted in Map 17 not recorded here.

SECTION 4

Aire-sur-l'Adour to the Pyrenees

From here until Arzacq-Arraziguet (after which you enter the département of the Pyrénées-Atlantiques) the route is waymarked with blue and yellow shell stickers, as well as with the familiar red and white balises.

After crossing the bridge KSO(R) ahead along (pedestrianised) **Rue Carnot** *(turn L part-way up for the cathedral and AP)*. At end turn R into **Rue Henri Labeyre** *(note brick building on RH side of street, former religious courts of justice and the 19th-century octagonal Halle aux Grains to R)* and then, at beginning of **Avenue des Pyrénées**, fork L up **Rue Félix Despagnet** *(passing gîte at no 21)* and the **Rue du Mas**, to the **Eglise de Sainte Quitterie**.

Continue to the end of the **Rue du Mas**, KSO ahead (**Avenue des Pyrénées)** then, opposite petrol station *(bar)* cross to RH side and KSO to end. At large roundabout turn R onto D2 (**Rue Nelson Mandela**) for 150m then turn L into **Rue Georges Fraisse** and L again along **Rue du Jardinet**. Turn R at end onto minor road leading down to a large reservoir, the **Retenue de Brousseau**

Here you would normally continue ahead along the LH side of the reservoir but when this edition was being prepared (summer 2009) large-scale repair works were underway on this bank, necessitating a (well waymarked) detour, described here. (However, If this is no longer the case when you use this guide follow the waymarks in place at the time and you will pick up the normal GR65 further on at *).

Turn hard R when you reach the reservoir along a grassy path, go down some steps and turn L onto an embankment, alongside lake. At end turn R onto minor road then 150m later reach a busy road and turn L uphill. Go under bridge under motorway and at top, 600m later, turn L by large factory building and then R (marked 'Lourine'). KSO. KSO at two crossroads, KSO ahead at LH turn, and at staggered crossing KSO(R) and then L ahead to hamlet of **Bégorre**. KSO, veering L, and 500m after hamlet turn R onto gravel track between fields.*

There are very few distinguishing features in this region, which is flat, with large-scale agriculture. Due to remembrement – *the regrouping of small, uneconomic portions of land into larger, more viable units – this whole area now consists of geometrically laid-out fields with irrigation channels and few hedge boundaries.*

About 200m later turn L onto similar track and KSO for 2km to D62. Turn R here then L almost immediately onto another similar track.

Turn L after 1km then immediately R. Just 600m later turn L again, watch out for RH fork R (preparations for new road building were in place in 2009) and then turn L by modern wayside cross to the D62 in…

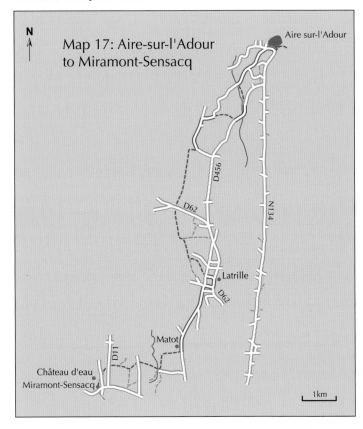

N

Map 17: Aire-sur-l'Adour to Miramont-Sensacq

Aire sur-l'Adour

D456

N134

D62

Latrille

D62

Matot

D11

Château d'eau
Miramont-Sensacq

1km

13.5km Latrille (596.5/141.5)

⚑ in churchyard, phone box, picnic area by church.

Continue past church onto D62 (**Route de Saint-Agnet**) then R again on D375 (**Rue des Sorbets**) and first L onto a minor road (**Chemin de Saint-Pé**). KSO for 2km passing **Matot** (farm, to R) then turn R at T-junction 100m later, which > grassy track. Follow it round for 1.5km then at another T-junction turn R onto grassy lane alongside a small river (the **Bahus**) to your L. Cross concrete FB and

KSO uphill, reaching minor road by farm. KSO ahead and 300m later, at crossing with another minor road, KSO ahead on gravel track through fields for 1km to the D11. Cross over, go up minor road on other side and turn L at junction *(seat)* into village. *(Turn R here for CH at La Maison du Bos, 05.58.79.93.18 & 06.81.59.87.80)*. Fork R 100m later towards château and church (on R) and go downhill into centre of…

6km Miramont-Sensacq 602.5/135.5)

Gîte d'étape communal, run by volunteers from the Association landaise des Amis de Saint-Jacques (05.58.79.94.06, all year but reserve October–April, 05.58.79.91.23, K). Hotel-restaurant Beaumont (05.58.79.90.65, closed weekends). 2 bakeries/limited groceries, ♣ opposite church.

Turn L along side of **Foyer Rural**, cross small square and turn R past Mairie *(gîte d'étape next door)* to junction with D314 (marked 'Lauret, Pimbo') and turn L along it. KSO for 2km and turn R opposite farm (**Jamboué-de-la-Lande**) onto minor road.

Turn R, turn R at T-junction, pass two farms, and road > green lane, descending gradually to valley bottom. Veer L to cross stream by FB, enter woods and

Map 18: Miramont-Sensacq to Boucoue

Eglise de Sensacq, total immersion font for infants

200m later KSO ahead along track coming from back L. About 150m later KSO ahead along unsurfaced track coming from L. KSO when another minor road joins from back L. Cross bridge and 150m later at road turn R to the…

4.5km Eglise de Sensacq 149m (607/131)

11th-century church formerly dedicated to St James. Contains total immersion font (for infants) in northwest corner. Completely enclosed porch, vestibule style, with some benches (useful for rest).

After visiting church the GR65 continues R ahead up minor road. About 700m later turn L up stony track to continue on GR, which leads you to the D111 1km later (*or KSO for 300m if you want to go to the Accueil à la Ferme with gîte at the Ferme de Marsan, Quartier Bestit, 05.58.79.94.93, 10pl, all year, K*). Turn R and then almost immediately L downhill through woods and then up, after 1.5km, into the centre of **Pimbo**.

*However, a more direct, shorter option is the old GR65 (no longer waymarked but very easy to follow). Return to junction (L) after visiting Eglise de Sensacq and KSO there, following road round uphill to D111 (1.5km). Turn L, passing hamlet of **Pibot**, and KSO for 1km more to…*

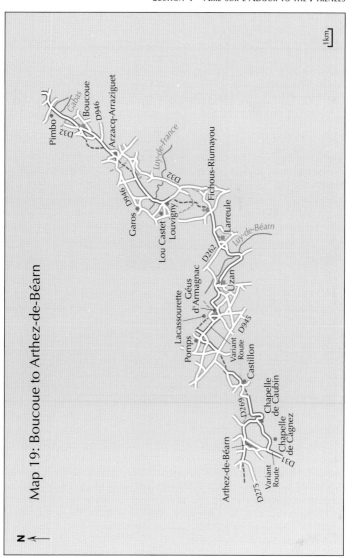

Map 19: Boucoue to Arthez-de-Béarn

159

4km Pimbo 190m (611/127)

Centre d'accueil communal next to church (05.58.44.46.57, open 10:00–18:00 Mon–Fri in season, 10:00–12:00 & 14:00–17:00 at other times, closed Sat & Sun, 4pl, 1/3–15/11, K). 2 CH, both on GR, both all year: a) 05.58.44.49.59 & 06.84.98.21.64), b) 05.58.44.46.92).

One of the oldest Bastide villages in the Landes, founded c1268, with collegiate church of Saint-Barthélmy on site of monastery founded by Charlemagne. ♣

If you took the main GR route, turn L through village and then fork R down road by wayside cross. If you took the *variante*, turn R to visit and then retrace your steps. Otherwise, turn hard L down road at entrance to village *(by wayside cross L, view of Arzacq-Arraziguet ahead on skyline)*.

Turn hard R 200m later *(seat to L with splendid views)* down track leading to valley bottom and KSO. Cross the river **Gabas** *(ivy-covered house on L has ♣ with drinking water outside)*. KSO at crossroads and after 2km reach crossing with D32 in **Boucoue**.

Here the GR65 turns hard R then immediately L up track leading to a farm (**Miquéou**) after 700m. Turn L here, veering R to a junction with another track and turn L to return to the D32. Turn R along it to the junction with the D946 (coming from back L). Alternatively, however, you can turn L along the road in **Boucoue** *(note style of chapel, L)* for 1.5km to junction.

In either case KSO ahead at junction along D946 for 1km *(FP to RH side to start with)*. Turn R uphill up **Côte de Camot** at entrance to town then L at top and follow road round, passing petrol station and supermarket into main square in…

7km Arzacq-Arraziguet 231m (618/120)

Superette, 2 bakeries, cafés, bank (+ATM). Gîte d'étape communal and campsite at Centre d'Accueil, Place du Marcadieu (05.59.04.41.41, meals possible, 36pl, all year, K, reservations recommended as used by a lot of groups). TO (Place de la République).

Bastide town with two main squares, side by side, founded by 'les Anglais' in 13th–14th centuries, Arzacq was in France at that time, not in the Béarn (a separate country); note names of rivers in the area: Luy-de-Béarn and Luy-de-France. Arzacq used to mark the boundary between France and the (then independent) Béarn country. Parish church of Saint-Pierre has stained-glass window of St James.

You have now left the département of Les Landes and entered the Pyrénées-Atlantiques. From here on churches along the route are very often closed, unlike those in the Haute Loire, Lozère, Aveyron, Lot, Tarn et Garonne, Gers and Landes, which are normally open all day long from Easter to November.

To continue, KSO ahead (one square to L, other to R) along small street (**Chemin de Saint-Jacques**) to R of bank. Turn L 100m later down walled lane, veering R, then turn L alongside large artificial lake. Just before the end (and before a deserted house) fork R onto grassy track leading around end of lake and along other side of it, turning L 300m later uphill into woods. Continue to road (400m) and turn R. *Note 'arbre du pèlerin' to R when you pass signboard for 'Vignes.' Good views over to the Pyrenees on a clear day.*

KSO for 2.5km (road > track), descending all the time to bridge over the **Luy-de-France**. Turn L by watermill (**Chemin du Moulin**) and 400m later turn second L (**Chemin de Fichous**) to church in…

4km Louvigny (622/116)

Modern church of St Martin replaces original church belonging to château formerly above the village in hamlet of Lou Castet; the remains of castle (dungeons) and church were demolished during the 20th century. One stained-glass window in new church contains *coquille* and pilgrim staff and gourd.

Continue on road to R of church then turn R uphill (**Chemin de Lassoulade**) 200m later up steep grassy lane to hamlet of **Lou Castet** *(site of former château)*. Turn L at T-junction and then fork L 400m later at junction (**Moundy**) up **Chemin de Pédebignes**, veering R very steeply uphill by new houses and continue ahead on ridge. *Splendid views on a clear day.*

KSO. KSO when stony track joins from back L, undulating at times, and ignoring turns, for 2.5km. At T-junction at end turn R and then KSO(R) ahead at junction 100m later, veering R downhill to valley bottom. Zigzag up on other side to emerge by Romanesque church in…

5km Fichous-Riumayou (627/111)

Phone box. CH, 15 Route de Fichous by school, continue on road for 200m after tennis courts (05.59.04.42.73 & 06.88.91.00.65).

Turn L by war memorial onto D279 (**Route de Fichous**) and 150m later turn R onto D278 (**Route de Larreule**). KSO downhill for 2km to...

2.5km Larreule (629.5/108.5)

Site of a Benedictine monastery founded about AD995 which was an important pilgrim stage in the Middle Ages, with church of Saint-Pierre, partly Romanesque. (The name *Larreule* means '*La Règle*' in Gascon – reflecting monastic rule – and is also found elsewhere, near Maubouget on the Arles route and in La Réole on the Vézélay route.)

Turn L for 100m to visit church (**Chemin de l'Eglise**; *adjoining garden is a nice place for a rest*) then retrace your steps to continue.

Cross the D262 in centre of village and KSO ahead on **Route de Mazerolles**, veering R when **Chemin de l'Eglise** joins from back L. Cross the **Luy-de-Béarn** (again), KSO(L) on other side and fork R at top of hill onto **Route de Uzan**. Turn R at T-junction after farm and continue on this road for 2.5km more to junction by church in...

4km Uzan (633.5/104.5)

Gîte d'étape on GR in village (05.59.81.65.76, 7pl, April–Oct, K).

Church of Sainte-Quitterie, Fontaine Sainte-Quitterie (a saint very revered in the area) on other side of road.

Turn R on D49 for 100m, turn R again and 100m later turn L onto minor road (*gîte at 1st house on L*) marked 'Géus', veering R. Turn L at large wayside cross, veering L, and 100m later turn R. Turn L at end by barn (*seat*) and KSO. Cross bridge over river **Ayguelongue** (*seat*) and continue to end of **Cami de la Lebe** in...

1.5km Géus (635/103)

a) Main GR65: turn R to **Chapelle de Géus** then turn L alongside Mairie (*large, shady grassed area with seats beside it*) on **Cami de Compostelle** (*large shady grassed area with seats by Mairie*). About 500m later at farm (**Lacassourette**) road > track and 200m later KSO(L) ahead, at bend, on grassy lane. KSO for 1km until you reach a road and turn R along it into **Pomps**.

b) Variante (useful in bad weather or if you are in a hurry): KSO here to junction 300m later then turn *second* R (**Route de Pomps**). KSO for 2km to...

2.5km Pomps (637.5/100.5)

Gîte d'étape communal (06.84.91.94.00 & 06.32.78.14.81,18pl, Mar–Nov, L). Bar/restaurant, shop (X Sun).

17th-century church of Saint-Jacques (with statue of the saint), château with octagonal tower.

At wayside cross turn R for bar/restaurant and church but KSO ahead for shop and gîte. To continue, turn L on **Rue de Caneigut** then R on **Route de Géus** and 150m later, after bridge, turn L on minor road, **Route de Brana**, veering R. Turn R at junction onto another minor road (**Route du Pèbe**) leading to D945 (1.5km from centre of Pomps).

Cross over, marked 'C2, Doazon,' and 150m later, after houses, fork R down track which disintegrates to FP (often overgrown but easy enough to follow as it goes in a straight line all the time). Turn R at end, after 1km, to D269 by bridge over the **Lech**. Turn L and follow road round to L after second bridge and then up to the village of **Castillon**, visible 2km away in front of you on top of the hill.

4.5km Castillon 198m (642/96)

Hospital for pilgrims and travellers in 11th century, church of Saint-Pierre.

Turn L at church and then, at junction with large wayside cross, KSO ahead down minor road which > a green lane after farm (**Lacoume**). Rejoin road (D269) again after 800m and KSO(L) ahead for 1km. Turn L (**Chemin de Benicet**) and KSO for nearly 1km to the D276. Turn R and 250m ahead of you on the LH side is the…

3km Chapelle de Caubin (645/93)

Restored Romanesque chapel on the site of the remains of a former Commandery of the Knights of St John. Garden opposite (picnic tables) contains a sculpture recalling the passage of pilgrims en route to Santiago.

Continue on road, uphill, and 100m later you have a choice:
   a) KSO ahead into **Arthez-de-Béarn** or
   b) turn L for the 10km *variante* route (not waymarked but easy to follow) which goes via the **Chapelle de Cagnez** and the **Cami Salié** (old salt route) and rejoins the main GR65 after the church in Argagnon, 1.5km before Maslacq. *For a description of this option see page 166.*

Corncobs drying in the Landes

2km Arthez-de-Béarn 211m (647/91)

Shop (X Sun), cafés, restaurant (no hotel). Gîte d'étape communal La Maison des Pèlerins (05.59.67.70.52, 20pl, all year, K), right at end of village, past church. Gîte-boulangerie Broussé (05.59.67.74.46, 8pl, all year, X Sun pm and Mon, meals for pilgrims if restaurant closed, K). 3 CH.

A very long town along a ridge (nearly 2km from one end to the other), originally developed around the Augustinian commandery whose monastery was destroyed in the Wars of Religion. Several interesting old houses, ramparts. Note transition towards Basque-style architecture.

Enter the town along the **Route de Caubin** and continue along the **Rue de Begoue**. Pass Mairie (on R) and KSO. When D946 turns R (to Orthez) KSO(L) ahead (**Rue du Bourdalet**) marked 'Gendarmerie', on ridge. At fork 500m later, with large wayside cross, fork R along **Chemin du Bosc**, along a ridge all the time, with superb views on a clear day *(the Pyrenees are over to your L in the distance)*.

KSO. Road > gravel track after a while. Continue for 3.5km then, 400m after passing under HT cables, 4.5km from church in Arthez, reach bend in small tarmac road (this is the **Route Impériale**) by house ahead (**Lasserre**) and fork L on it, downhill (**Route de l'Eglise**). Follow road down for 2.5km, passing various farms. Turn R at crossroads by house no 1857. KSO at next crossing 1km later *(bar/tabac signposted to R)* and reach bend in N117 by the…

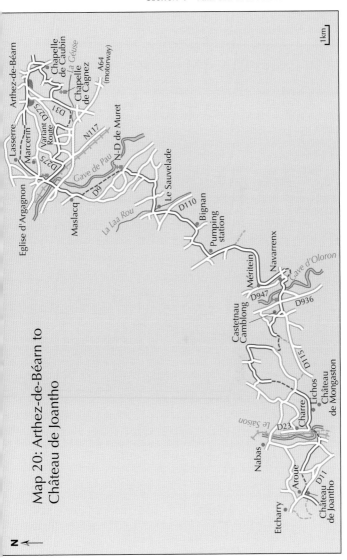

Map 20: Arthez-de-Béarn to Château de Joantho

N ←

1km

Arthez-de-Béarn
Chapelle de Caubin
La Géüse
Chapelle de Cagnez
A64 (motorway)
Lasserre
Marcerin
Variant Route
D31
D275
D275
Eglise d'Argagnon
N117
N-D de Muret
Gave de Pau
Le Sauvelade
Maslacq
D9
La Laa Rou
D110
Bignan
Pumping station
Mériteiñ
Navarrenx
Castetnau Camblong
Gave d'Oloron
D947
D936
D115
Lichos
Château de Mongaston
Charre
Le Saison
D23
Nabas
Aroue
D11
Etcharry
Château de Joantho

165

7km Eglise d'Argagnon (654/84)
Camping-Restaurant La Bulle, all year.

If you happen to arrive here at noon you will hear the Angelus *being rung, as you may have already in several other places along the route, at 7 o'clock in the morning and 7 o'clock at night as well. The name comes from the first word of the Latin text of a devotional office commemorating the Incarnation, and was said morning, noon and night, the bell being rung to announce it. Nowadays that is all that is left of the practice.*

Turn L along small FP to LH side of D117 to avoid a *lot* of very fast traffic, and just past the turn (R) to **Maslacq** cross over to other side of road then turn R to return to junction and then turn L onto the D275 ('Maslacq 2'). *(This is the* lieu-dit **Maysonnave**, *where the* variante *rejoins the main route from the L).*

Cross the railway line, the **Gave de Pau** (river) and the A64 motorway and KSO to village of **Maslacq**.

Cami Salié variante
About 100m after the **Chapelle de Caubin** turn L off D233 onto very minor road leading through woods to the **Chapelle de Cagnez**.

Built in the 11th–12th centuries this was formerly a parish church, important at a time when the pilgrim route led south to ford the Gave de Pau at a crossing place just below the Sanctuaire de Muret.

After visiting the church retrace your steps for 100m and then turn L on a track leading to D31 after 1km. Turn L along it for 1km and after wood (to L) and gas post on R turn R onto gravel track. About 1km later reach T-junction with tarred road, turn R for 500m then L onto the **Cami Salié**, *route used in former times for transporting salt, produced further west in Saliés-de-Béarn.*

Continue on it for 2km, along the side of the hill, until you reach the D275. Turn R here for 400m then, at a small junction, turn L onto a track. KSO for 1km and rejoin the main GR65 at the *lieu-dit* **Maysonnave** on the N117, just before its junction with the D275.

2km Maslacq (656/82)
Gite d'étape (ask in Epicerie-bar Pereira, X Wed, all day & Sun pm, 05.59.67.30.27 & 06.24.64.42.80, 6pl, all year, K). Hôtel/restaurant Maugouber (05.59.38.78.90, reservation needed).

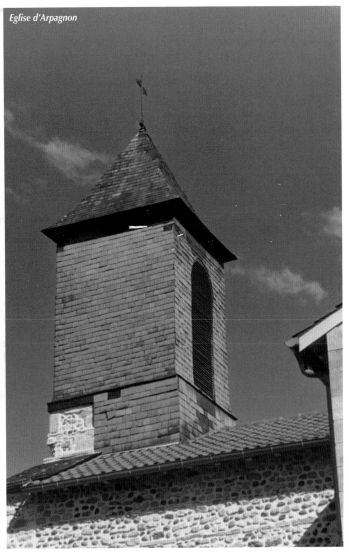

Eglise d'Arpagnon

Turn L (C9, Lagor) to continue on **Rue du Fronton**, passing *fronton. (Turn R fo shop, hotel and gîte.)* Turn L again opposite château onto the D9. About 300m later cross bridge over the **Géü** *(shady picnic area)* and turn L onto a minor road by a bus shelter. Fork L 300m later onto gravel track through fields and 300m after that, after bend turn R onto similar track. Cross minor road and KSO toward woods ahead, more or less // to river (**Gave de Pau** on your L). Continue uphill through woods (**Chemin de Girault Naule**), emerging at a crossing near the…

4km Sanctuaire de Notre-Dame de Muret (660/78)

Neo-Byzantine oratory, 1936, on site of 11th-century sanctuary. To visit, turn hard L for 300m.

To continue, KSO to D9 (200–300m). *The 'monster' in the valley below L is the Usine de Lacq, one of France's biggest natural gas works, resembling lighted candles on a giant industrial birthday cake...*

   Cross over, turn L behind house (**Chemin Bernadet**) and then L 100m late down minor road (**Chemin Bernadet**) then turn R 100m after that on **Chemin Saubade** to valley bottom. KSO over bridge at fork. KSO(R) at next fork, KSO(L) ahead at next (**Chemin de la Coume**) and continue to farm (**Haut-de-la-Coume**). Pass between buildings and continue on grassy track at edge of wood (field to R). Follow edge of woods round to L, enter woods, cross stream over FB. Go through (electric) fence and turn R, following it uphill, veering L alongside a line of trees to reach gravel lane to R of farm at **Larqué**. Turn R along it and 150m later at crossing (♣, seat) turn R along road, leading down and then steeply uphill. At top (a ridge) cross another road and go straight downhill on other side for 1km, veering R and then L to…

4km La Sauvelade (664/74)

Gîte-Café-Epicerie-Restaurant (05.59.67.33.69, 05.59.67.60.59 and 05.59.67.61.32, 16pl, 7/7 June–August, otherwise X Wed if not reserved, K). CH Les Campanhas, 280 Camin de la Crotz de Loupin (05.59.67.60.57).

   The church is all that remains of the monastery, originally Benedictine (and later Cistercian), founded by Gaston IV of Béarn in 1128. It was sacked by the Huguenots in 1569, restored after 1630 and then sold at the time of the French Revolution. The church was built between 1215 and 1250, originally dedicated to St Mary, but later changed to St James the Great in recognition of all the pilgrims who rested in the abbey. Statue of St James inside.

Turn L along D110 (**Route de Larvath**) for 1km, passing Mairie, then fork R uphill (*Camin de Compostela, D110 continues L*) and KSO for 3km. At the very top (**Hameu de Bignon**, *seat*), opposite a large restored house, turn R along a road coming from the L (**Camin de Berduguen**). Continue on ridge for 600m then fork L (still the **Camin de Berduguen**) and 300m later turn L, downhill at junction marked 'ancienne école' to cross the river **Saleys**. Continue uphill for 1.5km to a T-junction with a road running at right angles along a ridge *(former school to R, small water tower in front)*.

Turn L along the ridge, KSO for 1.5km then turn second R down a minor road. *(Splendid views over to the Pyrenees in clear weather.)* KSO for 3.5km, downhill through woods and then along the level. KSO(L) (**Camin dous Barrets**, > **Camin Clavarette**) at fork in residential area then turn L after crossing small bridge and continue to church in…

11km Méritein (675/63)

About 500m later, at church (R), turn L for 50m then L again down a minor road, **Chemin de la Biasse**, with fields to either side, for 1.5km. Cross another road via a tunnel underneath it then KSO to junction with the D111. Turn R, cross bridge over river, continue and cross **Avenue de Mourenx** and KSO on other side (**Rue de la Batteuse**) between former petrol station (L) and ramparts (R).

Turn R *(PTT now on your L)* and continue down **Rue Saint-Germain**, turning L into **Place Carrérot** to the **Eglise Saint-Germain** in…

2km Navarrenx 125m (677/61)

Population 1500. Shops, cafés, restaurants. Accueil pèlerins (18:00, in church, 18:30 *verre d'amitié* in presbytery, 17:30 Sat, Easter to 1/11). Gîtes d'étape communaux (05.59.66.10.22, 16 & 19pl, all year, K. Keys from Bar Le Dahu, 23 Rue Saint-German until 18:00, 05.59.66.02.67). CH Le Relais du Jacquet, 42 Rue Saint-Germain (06.75.72.89.33). Bar des Sports, Rue Saint-Antoine, has rooms (05.59.66.50.63). Hôtel-restaurant du Commerce (05.59.66.50.16). Camping-snack Beau Rivage, Allée des Marronniers by river (15/3–15/10). TO (Rue Saint-Germain, Arsenal).

First town in France to be fortified with Italian-style ramparts (16th century); ask at TO for town plan with walking tour. Church of Saint-Germain, finished 1562, but rapidly converted into a Protestant *temple* under the

▶

orders of Jeanne d'Albret, remaining so until 1620 when it was reconverted to a Catholic church (note pilgrim boss in ceiling near side chapel to RH side, with head with leather hat and *coquille*). In former times Navarrenx also had a significant *Cagot* (outcast) population (see page 144), many of whom became prominent public figures in the early 20th century.

To continue, with your back to the church and **Place Darralde** KSO(L) ahead down **Rue Saint-Antoine** into the **Place Caserne** and then turn L to go through the **Porte Saint-Antoine** and continue down to cross the bridge over the **Gave d'Oloron** (river). Gîte Gave et Remparts 300m after bridge, on GR *(05.59.66.08.93 & 06.24.34.55.13,all year, K)*.

Cross bridge, turn R onto D115 on other side (**Avenue de la Gare**). Cross roundabout, continue ahead on other side (**Route de la Chapelle**) and 500m later turn R, marked 'Centre Bourg', into the lower part of…

2.5km Castetnau-Camblong (679.5/58.5)

Gîte, 21 Rue du Bourg (05.59.66.50.73 & 06.71.55.22.38, all year, K). CH Maison Lespoune (05.59.66.24.14). Supermarket at 9 Route de Bayonne.

Castetnau = '*villeneuve*' in Béarnais, Camblong = '*le champ long*'. 17th--century church, note Béarn-style houses.

Turn R at T-junction, pass church (on your R) and 100m later turn L down minor road (**Rue de Débantets**) to T-junction (approx 600m) with wayside cross. Turn L onto unsurfaced road through forest, descending to cross the **Pont de Camblong** over the **Lausset** (1km).

About 100m later turn R at crossing of tracks and KSO, through woods uphill (800m). At junction turn R over stream then 100m later turn hard R on better track *(back downhill again, a manoeuvre necessitated by not being able to go through private land)*. Track joins from back R. KSO and cross wooden bridge over the **Harcelanne**. About 150m later reach minor road. Turn L for 1.2km then turn R up grassy track, forking L 50m later and veering R and then L uphill.

Continue ahead uphill, through fields, veering R again and > track and reach T-junction (1.5km). Turn L, descend to cross the **Cassol du Boué** (small river), pass to R of large shed and then veer L uphill on stony track to a crossroads with the D115 (1km after stream). *On the other side of the road the Jean Haget pâté manu-facturer has erected a covered rest area with picnic tables for pilgrims and walkers, with some of their products for sale.* Turn R then immediately L (the **Route de Saint-Jacques**, marked 'Château de Mongaston') onto minor road (D343) and

SECTION 4 – AIRE-SUR-L'ADOUR TO THE PYRENEES

go downhill for 2km to bridge over the **Apaure** *(picnic tables)*. KSO ahead. Just 400m later pass entrance road (L) to…

9.5km Château de Mongaston (689/49)

Castle built in the 13th century by Gaston IV of Béarn, destroyed by fire 1929 and now restored by its present owner. Visits 1/5–30/10 X Tues, 14:30–18:00).

Continue on road and 500m later turn R (**Route du Saison**) in hamlet of **Cherbeys**. About 300m later turn L by entrance boards for **Charre** then 600m after that cross the D23. Go over cattle grid and turn L onto track // to road, with fields to R. Around 300m later return to D23 (L) and on FP alongside it reach road bridge over the river **Saison**. Turn R over it immediately and then fork R on other side down a slope onto minor road veering R to village of **Lichos** *(birthplace of Saint-Grat, Bishop of Oloron. 2 CH: a) Maison Carrère, by church (05.59.28.81.78), b) Maison Montalibet, next to Mairie (05.59.28.85.63 & 06.24.06.57.07).* Turn L at junction, then R at wayside cross, veer L and then R to cross bridge over river **Borlaas** *(seats).* KSO, cross a road and KSO ahead on minor road for 1.8km, uphill.

Just after farm to R (**Bouhaben** – *gîte d'étape privé, 05.59.65.70.19 & 06.16.48.73.65, 10pl, all year, K)* and before LH bend, KSO(R) at fork and continue ahead up grassy lane. KSO(L) at fork, go through gate into meadow and continue alongside hedge to L then turn R down towards house. This is the **Maison Bellerive** (Belabua), with another gîte d'étape privé *(05.59.65.70.19 & 06.16.48.73.65, 10pl, all year, K).* Go through large metal gate, go past house and then down tarred lane to D11 *(500m, Accueil à la Ferme opposite at Ferme Behoteguya, 05.59.65.85.69, gîte for pilgrims only, 6pl, meals, RE, April–Oct after 14:00).* KSO(R) along it for 600m to the…

6km Château de Joantho (695/43)

18th-century manor house, privately owned.

However, to continue into **Aroue** KSO ahead for 500m. Small gîte d'étape communal 150m before church on L (05.59.65.95.54, 12pl, April–Nov, K). Romanesque church of St Etienne has 12th-century bas-reliefs with Santiago Matamoros ('the Moor-slayer') in lintel in sacristy doors.

To continue you have a choice of two waymarked routes:
   a) Main GR65: *This is a high-level route, with splendid views on a clear day,*

Eglise d'Olhaïby

but it does not pass the Eglise d'Olhaïby directly. Turn L down a minor road along side **Château de Joantho** and KSO for 2km. Then, at a junction just before a RH bend and LH fork, turn R up a gravel lane, steeply uphill. KSO then continue on ridge, up and down, 'on the roof of the world' style. Around 2km later, by isolated stone barn, do NOT turn L on route waymarked in yellow but KSO ahead. About 600m later reach large house by minor road and turn hard L downhill.

Some 800m later reach minor road by another isolated stone barn and turn R; 500m later either turn L straightaway to continue or KSO ahead to the **Eglise d'Olhaïby** and then retrace your steps to the junction.

b) The variant route (waymarked) continues on the D11 through Aroue and takes you directly to the church in Olhaïby.

5km Eglise d'Olhaïby (700/38)

Simple Romanesque church of Saint-Just (not always open but large, covered porch is a good place for rest/shelter).

Retrace your steps to junction then KSO(R) ahead on minor road for 1km, ignoring turns (road > track after 1km). KSO, turn R on road by farm (**Etcheberria**) and then veer L to another farm (**Jaurriberria**). Turn hard L onto wide gravel lane and pass to L of it and continue uphill on wide lane onto plateau (**Archelako**) and KSO, ignoring turnings, on ridge. About 2.5km later (after Jaurriberria) turn R at T-junction with 'balcony' view of landscape ahead to the…

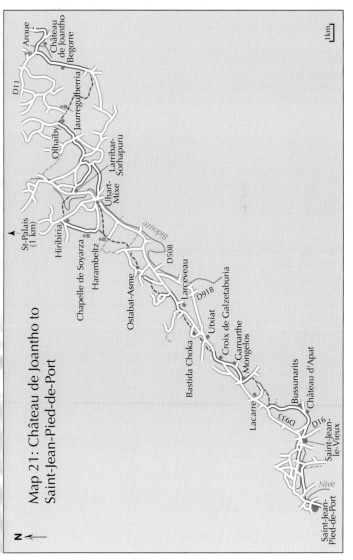

Map 21: Château de Joantho to
Saint-Jean-Pied-de-Port

N ←

Aroue
Château
de Joantho
Begorre
D11
Jaurreguberria
Olhaïby
Larribar-
Sorhapuru
Uhart-
Mixe
St-Palais
(1 km)
Hiribiria
Chapelle de Soyarza
Harambeltz
Ostabat-Asme
Bidouze
D508
Larceveau
D918
Bastida Choka
Utxiat
Croix de Galzetaburia
Gamarthe
Mongelos
Lacarre
D933
Bussunarits
Château d'Apat
D16
Saint-Jean-
le-Vieux
Nive
Saint-Jean-
Pied-de-Port

1 km

4km Ferme de Benta (704/34)

If you want to go to **Saint-Palais** (7km, *Donapaleu* in Basque), the capital of the Basque province of *Basse-Navarre (to continue in Spain along the Camino del Norte, for example, see Appendix B)* KSO ahead 100m later at farm on minor road to **Quinquilenia**, continuing through **Uruxondoa** and **Béhasque-Lapiste** *(Gîte Uhaldia (05.59.65.75.80 & 06.32.10.95.87, 8pl, all year, K),* turning L onto the D11 to Saint-Palais at **Quintalena**.

St-Palais *Population 2000, all facilities. Gîte d'étape in Maison Franciscaine, Avenue de Gibraltar, on way out of town leading back to GR65 (05.59.65.90.77, 48pl, Easter–1/11, K), run by volunteers from the Association des Amis de Saint-Jacques des Pyrénées Atlantiques. Three hotels, 6 restaurants. Camping-bar-snack municipal Ur Alde (on D933 500m out of town towards Aîciritz, chalets + K also available, 15/4–15/10). TO (14 Place Charles de Gaulle). Musée de la Basse Navarre et des Chemins de Saint Jacques de Compostelle, next to Mairie.*

You can pick up the GR65 again at **Hiriburia** by taking the D302 south and either continuing on the road or taking the turning L onto the Vézelay route.

Otherwise, to continue, turn L (farm to L) 100m later down minor road, steeply downhill. KSO, KSO(L) at fork and KSO, ignoring turns, for 1km then turn R along D242 for 400m. *Here you have two options: the 2km longer, main GR via Larribar-Sorhapuru to Harambeltz or the short-cut route via Uhart-Mixe but which misses out both the Chapelle de Soyarza and Hiriburia, where the routes from Paris/Tours, Vézelay and Le Puy all meet up to form a single Chemin de Saint-Jacques into Spain.*

a) Main GR65: continue ahead on the D242 for 600m more then turn L along C2 ('Larribar 1,2') for 1km then veer L at *fronton*, L to church, cross bridge over D933 and then KSO down minor road in...

4km Larribar-Sorhapuru 89m (708/30)

Veer R between two farms and continue downhill to cross four-arched bridge over the **Bidouze**. *(Note shrine to R with small statue of St James behind glass in a 'stèle' and also watercolour of church under glass.)*

At a T-junction turn L onto grassy track, enter woods and track > FP with rocky 'steps', becoming narrower as you climb. When it levels out, veer L and path > wider. Go through 'gate', continue along narrow FP between hedges, gradually widening out, and reach road at farm.

2km Hiriburia 151m (710/28)

A few metres to the R, where the routes from Paris, Vézélay and Le Puy are thought to have met, the Société des Amis de Saint Jacques have erected a small monument. (You can also go to Saint-Palais from here: KSO(R) for 3km.) If you look at the monument's 'feet' and follow the direction pointed by those marked 'Ostabat' you will also see where you are going next: up the clear track uphill in front of you, the 'Chemin de Procession' leading to the chapel.

To continue, KSO ahead for 100m then cross the D302 and turn L up the **Chemin de Procession** leading up to the **Chapelle de Soyarza**, *300m, a modern building replacing a much older oratory dedicated to Notre-Dame. Adjoining the chapel is a covered rest area with pilgrim book. Superb views all round from the top on a clear day.*

Continue downhill on the other side on a wide track, veering L alongside woods. About 800m later, 100m past modern shrine (L), turn R down clear grassy track, veering L to join track coming from back L. Veer R then L downhill to village of **Harambeltz**.

b) Short-cut via Uhart-Mixe: turn L at next junction (ie after 400m on the D242) and then immediately R *(here you will see the first 'snail' waymark)* very

Meeting point of three French routes, Hiriburia

steeply uphill, which > a gravel road after farm buildings. KSO, undulating between fields, and 400m later cross minor road. *(Turn L here for gîte d'étape privé at the Ferme Arosteguia, 05.59.65.27.94 & 06.27.71.69.82, 14pl, Mar–Oct, RE)*. KSO ahead, downhill. Pass farm, veering R and then L and KSO, ignoring turnings. Reach the D302, turn R over two road bridges over the river **Bidouze** and reach junction with the D933 by the church in…

4km Uhart-Mixe

Bar Ostatua Café Duhalde (05.59.65.60.00 & 06.16.33.72.13, 15/3–15/10, 7/7) has rooms, gîte d'étape L'Escargot (4pl), refuge (donation), camping (donation) and does light meals.

Cross D933 and continue on other side by Mairie (L), steeply uphill *(waymarked in this section with red arrows)*. Turn (not fork) L at top by wayside cross and KSO. KSO(L) at fork and KSO. Pass another wayside cross (L) by junction and KSO ahead, uphill.

At the top, at a four-way junction, the main GR65 joins from above R (forking down), marked (pointing uphill) 'Chapelle de Soyarza'. KSO ahead here, though, marked 'Harambeltz, Ostabat'. KSO downhill and 600m later turn R into the village of…

3km Harambeltz (713/25)

Site of former Benedictine priory–hospital of Saint-Nicholas. The 1000-year-old chapel remains and has an 18th-century altarpiece and statue of St James, but belongs to the families in the village and is not a parish church. It is difficult to visit, though the *grille* (but not the door) is sometimes open, enabling you to see inside. (In the process of being restored in 2009.) Note interesting old houses in the village.

KSO(R) down main street, pass to L of church, KSO ahead under trees at LH bend, veering R and then L downhill immediately on FP veering R at bottom to cross stream. On other side track is wider; KSO up it, ignoring turns until you emerge from the woods at a T-junction with a track (1.5km). Turn L and go downhill, veer L at bottom then R and follow road round ignoring turns. Pass **Lagunatona** *(group of houses)* and at crossroads KSO. About 200m later fork L down grassy track *(sculpture at start)* which > walled lane into village of…

4km Ostabat-Asme (Izura) 124m (717/21)

Gîte d'Etape Maison Ospitalia in lower part of town (05.59.37.83.17 & 06.10.04.65.75, 10pl, 12/4–31/10, K). CH Auberge Ametzanea (05.59.37.85.03 X Sun) Two bars (one with shop, X Thurs), one with restaurant.

Ostabat is a small village today, but in the past it was an important gathering point for pilgrims coming along different routes. In the Middle Ages its hospitals and inns could accommodate up to 5000 pilgrims, but only the Maison Ospitalia remains and is now the *gîte d'étape*.

There are no big pilgrim monuments in the French Basque country, but there were formerly many small hospitals and chapels (in Harambeltz and Itziat, for example).

Pass *gite d'étape*, turn R uphill to village centre (Mairie, church) then veer L on road out of village. KSO at crossing and KSO on tarred lane leading uphill *(Gîte d'étape + CH at Ferme Gaineko-Extea 800m later, 05.59.37.81.10 & 06.72.73.78.56, gîte 19 + 14pl, 1/4–15/10 from 14:00; open Nov–Mar if reserved)*. KSO(L) ahead at bend by farm on shady lane. Around 1km later KSO at crossing with large concrete wayside cross and KSO ahead. Pass farm, track > tarmac road and at junction with another road coming from back R KSO(L) ahead. Turn L at crossing by farm and reach the D933. Turn R along it for 300m (FP on LH side) then turn R up tarmac lane, veering L to T-junction *(bakery/shop 60m to L)* on the edge of…

3.5km Larceveau 160m (720.5/17.5)

Hotel-restaurant Espellet (05.59.37.81.91, 7/7), on main road. Gîte Pagolateia, Quartier Bastida-Xoto (06.73.35.20.93, all year, K). Restaurant (7/7 in season, otherwise X Sun evening and Mon). Bakery (X Tues. in winter).

From here to Saint-Jean-Pied-de-Port you are following the D933 along the valley all the time, mainly on old lanes, on one side of the main road or the other.

Turn R here up minor road, veering L to continue // to D933 below. Just before the hamlet of **Chahara** (main road now 100m to L). KSO at crossroads with electricity substation and go through hamlet, passing to R of large house and continue ahead on lane between fences. Turn L at minor road and 50m later turn R onto green lane.

Join minor road coming from L and KSO(R) ahead, veering L past farm in hamlet of **Bastida-Choko**. About 300m later, just after houses, continue ahead on grassy track to cross stream and then turn L alongside it, returning to D933 again. Turn R along FP alongside but above road and in hamlet of **Utziat** *(there was a hospital for pilgrims here in the 12th century and you pass the former mill attached to it)*. KSO ahead along minor road in front. Veer R and almost immediately turn L through gateway, to continue alongside hedge to your R. (You are now // to road again.) Follow the hedge, pass inside the edge of a wood and then above vines before returning to the D933 again (1km). KSO along road for 300m to a roadside cross (R), the…

5.5km Croix de Galzetaburia 262m (726/12)

This cross (1714; the name means '*tête du chemin'*) was placed at this crossing of Roman roads where pilgrims from secondary routes joined the Via Podensis. It has Christ on one face, the Virgin and Child on the other, and two inscriptions on its base: a Latin hymn and a Basque text indicating that you are halfway between the Soule and the Labourd, two of the three Basque provinces in France.

Turn L down a minor road (D522) leading to the village of **Gamarthe** (1km). Turn hard L then hard R and continue through village, past church, veering R, and (pink) *fronton*.

Continue ahead on minor road out of village leading back to the D933 at **Mongelos**. Turn L along it for 100m then turn L down minor road. About 750m later turn R along another minor road. KSO at staggered junction then at the next junction turn L uphill. Cross *passage canadien* (cattle grid) and KSO, ignoring turns. Just before a second cattle grid, and 250m from the D933, turn hard L uphill, veering R. KSO, ignoring turns. Road > a wide track for a while and then a minor road again; follow it downhill in a large 'C' shaped loop all the time, ignoring turnings. Pass through the village of **Bussunarits** *(CH at Ferme Etxekonia, just off GR65 to L, 05.59.37.00.40)*, Join larger road coming from L at junction with very large, red wayside cross, just before the 11th-century **Château d'Apat**, cross bridge, veer R to crossroads and KSO ahead on smaller road. Veer R near end and emerge on the D18, turning R to church and main square in…

8km Saint-Jean-le-Vieux (Donazaharre) 212m (734/4)

Shop, cafés, restaurant. Hôtel-restaurant (05.59.37.11.81, 1/4–1/11). Gîte du Camp Romain, Maison Ur Bizia (05.59.49.16.54 & 06.86.99.82.03, all year).

Pilgrims originally went straight from Saint-Jean-le-Vieux to Saint-Michel (the route described in Aymery Picard's 12th-century guidebook). The deviation via Saint-Jean-Pied-de-Port developed from the 13th century onwards.

Church of Saint-Pierre, an example of a typically Basque church, with galleries on two levels around three sides of the nave. Until the 14th century it was affiliated to the Augustinian Canons in Roncesvalles. Musée archéologique.

With your back to the church and facing the *fronton* turn L at LH far corner of square onto a minor road. Veer L at bend, go under the D933 and turn L on other side. Turn L at crossroads (marked 'Madeleine') and 250m later turn L to D933. Turn R along it for 100m then turn L down tree-lined lane (marked 'La Magdaleine'). Some 150m later turn R down minor road between fields, leading through the *Quartier de la Madeleine (campsite to R, 1/4–15/10, 12–15pl in mobile homes, K)*. About 300–400m after campsite there is a CH *(6 Chemin Taillapalde, 05.59.37.09.74)*.

Pass *fronton* (L) and turn L down side of the **Eglise Sainte-Marie-Madeleine** *(the present building in pink stone replaces an earlier one)*. Cross the river **Laurhibar** and KSO, uphill to crossing with D401 (**Route de Caro**). Cross over, KSO up **Chemin Saint-Jacques**, go through the **Porte Saint-Jacques** and down the **Rue de la Citadelle** to the church (L) in…

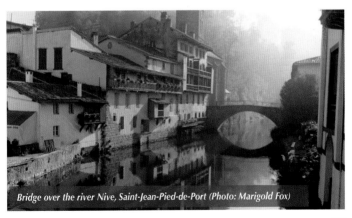

Bridge over the river Nive, Saint-Jean-Pied-de-Port (Photo: Marigold Fox)

4km Saint-Jean-Pied-de-Port (Donibarne Garazi) 180m (738/0)

Population 1400. All facilities. TO (14 Place De Gaulle). Accueil Pèlerin, Association des Amis de Saint-Jacques des Pyrénées Atlantiques (ASJPA), 39 Rue de la Citadelle (05.59.37.05.09, 15/3–15/11, 07:30–12:00 & 13.30–22.30). Refuge municipal, 39 Rue de la Citadelle (run by ASJPA, 24pl, no reservations, 15/3–1/11, K). Refuge de pèlerins Le Chemin vers l'Etoile, 21 Rue d'Espagne ((05.59.37.20.71, 20pl, all year). Refuge Esponda, Place du Trinquet (06.37.50.01.65, all year, K). Gîte d'Etape Zazpiak-bat, 13bis Route Maréchal Harispe (on GR65, 05.59.49.10.17 & 06.75.78.36.23, 18pl, all year). Gîte L'Esprit du Chemin, 40 Rue de la Citadelle (05.59.37.24.68, 18pl, April–Sept), 5 hotels, 9 CH. 2 campsites a) Camping municipal Plaza Berri, Avenue du Fronton (1/4 –30/10), b) Camping de l'Arradoy, 4 chemin de Zalicarte (Mar–Sept). Pilgrim information office (Acceuil Pèlerin de l'Association des Amis de Saint-Jacques des Pyrénées Atlantiques) is run by volunteers, mainly former pilgrims, at 39 Rue de la Citadelle, open March–Nov, early morning to late evening, and provides information on the route in Spain and helps with accommodation; it is suggested you call there as soon as you arrive in St-Jean-Pied-de-Port. TO. SNCF (to Bayonne).

This is 'Saint John-at-the-Foot-of-the-Pass', a small border town on the river Nive, capital of the Basque province of Basse Navarre with an ancient cobbled *'haute ville'*. Several places of interest: Citadelle overlooking the town, built by Vauban, with its system of ramparts, accessed either from the top end of the Rue de la Citadelle or by staircase *('escalier de la poterne')* leading up from the footpath along the river by the side of the church – worth the climb on a clear day; Prison des Evêques; Musée de la Pelote; 14th-century Eglise Notre-Dame-du-bout-du-pont ('Our Lady at the end of the bridge', part of the former priory hospital); Pont Romain and the different *portes* (Saint-Jacques, d'Espagne, for example). Note architecture of Basque-style houses with often ornate wooden overhangs at roof level and balconies. If you have time to spare the TO has a booklet of waymarked walks in the area.

Traditionally pilgrims entered the town by the Porte Saint-Jacques at the top of the Rue de la Citadelle, and those who have followed the GR65 will have done the same. After that there were two routes to Roncesvalles. The older one, following the course of the river Valcarlos, is now the modern road (D933 in France, N135 in Spain). This route is also waymarked. It is no shorter, is far from flat but is not as high and if the weather is very bad or visibility poor you should take this.

The other, the high-level **Route Napoléon**, was the one he took to cross into Spain, following existing tracks used by shepherds and pilgrims for several centuries. It leads over the Pyrenees via the Col de Bentarte and the Porte de Cize, continuing along the path of the old Roman road from Bordeaux to Astorga, and is normally accessible without any trouble (such as too much snow) from May to October. It is 26km long and a spectacular route on a clear day, but do not attempt it if it is already very windy down below in Saint-Jean-Pied-de-Port; higher up you can experience force 9 gales and appalling weather, even in the height of summer.

The Route Napoléon was also the one favoured by pilgrims in centuries gone by. Although it was much more strenuous, it was also exposed for most of the way, and pilgrims were thus less likely to be ambushed by bandits than on the densely wooded route through Valcarlos. If you are a fairly fit walker allow at least seven hours' actual walking (excluding stops); if not, allow much longer, especially if it is windy (when it will almost always be against you).

If you do decide to take the high-level route you also have the option of continuing (very steeply) uphill for 5km after reaching Saint-Jean-Pied-de-Port to **Hunto** (500m) where there is a CH and *gîte d'étape* at the Ferme Ithuriburia (05.59.37.14.73, 21pl, all year, K) to shorten the stage to Roncesvalles or for 8km to the **Refuge-Auberge d'Orisson** (790m, 05.59.49.13.03 & 06.81.49.79.56, 18pl, meals, bar, 31/3–31/10). This should present no problems in summer but remember that the weather can be very bad (snow, thick fog, high winds) in the spring and autumn and that once you have committed yourself to this route you will either have to stick with it or retrace your steps back down to Saint-Jean-Pied-de-Port and then continue via Valcarlos.

Whichever route you take, though, and especially if you spend the night in Saint-Jean-Pied-de-Port, start early in the day (06:30 in summer, or as soon as it is light), not only to avoid the heat but also to avoid being high up later in the day when the light is fading and you are tired. If you choose the Route Napoléon **take enough food and water** with you, including (both routes) the following morning's breakfast and, if you do not want to eat in one of the restaurants in Roncesvalles, something for an evening meal. Descriptions of both alternatives are given in Appendix A.

APPENDIX A

Saint-Jean-Pied-de-Port to Roncesvalles

A. VALCARLOS ROUTE

From the **Rue de la Citadelle** go through the **Porte d'Espagne** (passing the church on your L, ♣), cross the bridge over the river **Nive**, go up the **Rue d'Espagne** but then turn R into the **Rue d'Uhart**. Continue along **Place Floquet** (under the *jardin public*), through the rampart gateway and then, after 20m, bear L when you see a signpost for the D933, marked 'Arnéguy 8'. Follow the road round for 1.5km then look out for a RH fork taking you down off the road towards a farm and then veering R to cross the bridge over the river **Nive**. Around 500m later reach a T-junction with a road coming from your R (from **Lasse**) and turn L here. KSO(L) ahead at fork 1km later and KSO(L) again at the next fork. Then KSO on this road, an old tarred lane in parts, that follows the **Nive** (to your L below), often at some considerable distance above it, up and down along the side of the hill. Continue ahead all the time (the route is very easy to follow) until you pass a hotel and come out on the Spanish side of the road bridge in the border town of...

8km Arnéguy

Bars, hotel, a lot of *ventas (originally country inns but nowadays duty-free-type shops)*.

KSO(R) on the D933 but watch out for waymarks that may take you off the road (*the walkers' route to Roncesvalles is very clearly marked off-road once you are in Spain*) to its LH side on a section of the D128 as far as Ondarolle, when you turn R to...

3km Valcarlos (Luzaïde) 365m

Border town on the Spanish side, with shops, TO, 2 banks (one with ATM), 2 hotels, pensión, bars and restaurants. Albergue municipal turístico (0034-948-79-01-17, 24pl, K). CH (0034-948-79-00-11 & 0034-609-43-61-90, + *gîtes ruraux* rented per night, 22pl).

Church of Santiago contains a life-size representation of Santiago Matamoros.

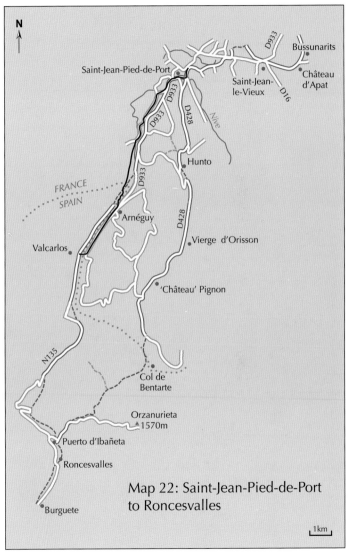

Map 22: Saint-Jean-Pied-de-Port to Roncesvalles

Roldán (Roland) monument, Puerto d'Ibañeta

Continue on the main road (*waymarked from time to time, both with yellow arrows and red-and-white* balises). There is a short, off-road section to the L before the hamlet of **Gañecolata** and then, just before the road KM 57 post, you fork L down a gravel track downhill, crossing an old stone bridge over a small river at the bottom.

Shortly after going through a gate watch out carefully, as you then leave the track (which continues to a farm at the end) and fork R uphill on a FP. This undulates along the side of the hill, with splendid views on a clear day.

When track goes uphill again fork hard R (by a *camino* bollard) then hard L up grassy lane, leading uphill.

When the line of electric pylons turn R, KSO(L) on forest track, veering R through beech woods, winding its way up to a junction of similar tracks (marked with another *camino* bollard). Turn L, veering R then L uphill to emerge on the main road again at a bend by a small farm.

Turn L and 50m later turn L down shady level lane through woods, rising gently at first and then more steeply as grassy track winds along the side of the hill, following the line of the electric pylons. This section is very easy to follow and brings you out on a minor road to L of the main road, just before the chapel and orientation table at the…

13km Puerto d'Ibañeta 1057m

As related in the 10th-century narrative poem *Chanson de Roland*, the hero of this name, Count of Brittany and Charlemagne's nephew, attempted to resist the rear guard of the Saracen army at a famous battle in the Pyrenees in 778, single-handed and with only his faithful sword Durendal to defend himself. Too proud to blow his horn (the *olifant*) to summon assistance as instructed, he only did so after he had been mortally wounded. The Puerto d'Ibañeta is where Charlemagne and his retreating army had got to when they heard the sound of Roland's horn – too late to go back to help him.

A bell used to toll at the original chapel to guide pilgrims in bad weather. The modern *ermita* (chapel) of San Salvador was built in 1965 to replace the earlier ruined chapel of Charlemagne, with a sign in French, Spanish, Basque and Latin inviting pilgrims to pray to Notre-Dame de Roncevaux. It is usually locked, but you can see inside through the apertures in the door; the interior is very plain but has some nice stained-glass windows, best seen with the sunlight behind them. Outside altar for outdoor masses. There is also a modern monument nearby to Roland (Roldán in Spanish).

* Cross road and go up mound ahead to chapel. From here you walk through the woods for the last 1.5km to Roncesvalles. With your back to the chapel go down FP to LH side of road and the RH side of a small white building and follow it gently downhill all the time. Shortly before you get to the abbey you are joined by a track coming from the back L, after which you enter the rear of the monastery. Turn R and then L under arch, go through a courtyard and pass in front of the church in **Roncesvalles**.

B. ROUTE NAPOLEON

The Route Napoléon is the continuation of the GR65 over the Pyrenees. It is now tarmacked as the D428 until just before the Col de Bentarte, but is normally very quiet, with little traffic except at weekends when the hunting season opens in October. It is clearly waymarked with yellow flashes and/or arrows (these 'flechas amarillas' will continue all through Spain too) with scallop shells as well as with the familiar red-and-while balises, and is easy to follow as you continue up the D428 all the time, ignoring turns, apart from a few occasions when you short-cut some of its many hairpins.

Go down the **Rue de la Citadelle**, past the church of **Notre-Dame-du-bout-du-Pont** (♣), through the **Porte d'Espagne**, cross the bridge over the river **Nive** and KSO on up the **Rue d'Espagne**. Continue ahead up the **Route Saint-Michel** for approx 100m, bear L at a fork and after 20m you will come to a junction with the **Route Maréchal Harrispe**. Take this (bear R off the **Route Saint-Michel**, which bends round to the L, ♣). KSO and after approximately 500m there is a small junction and the road name changes to **Route Napoléon**.

Follow the road as it winds (mostly up) and (sometimes) down, past small roadside farms. At fork bear L. KSO following road all the time *(but keep turning round from time to time to admire the view – after this there is nothing as steep until you climb up to O Cebreiro and enter Galicia). At this level there are still trees to provide some shade.*

Pass a T-junction (**Maison Etchébestia**, 302m), and KSO. About 100m further on, road forks at massive tree *(good place for a rest)*; keep R here *(fork to L goes down to village of Saint-Michel)* and KSO to...

5km Hunto 540m

Gîte d'étape/CH at the Ferme Ithurburia (05.59.37.11.17, 21pl in gîte, all year, K).

About 150m after passing Hunto the road veers R, but the GR65 bears L up a grassy track (the old road), leaving the modern road for a while (to rejoin it later) making a short cut via the old, steep route that zigzags between walls/banks at first and then on open ground. The path joins the (modern) road again (at 710m), after eight of nine hairpins, by two small houses L and R of the road – the one on the R is called **Arbol Azopian.** ♣ *to RH side and orientation table opposite.*

From here you can see over the mountains to the east towards the Col de Somport, Mont d'Aspe, and beyond, snow-covered (peaks) for much of the year.

KSO on road and pass the…

3km Refuge-Auberge Orisson 790m

Rooms (05.59.49.13.03 & 06.81.49.79.56, 18pl, 31/3–31/10), café restaurant open all day.

KSO on road again, ignoring tracks to either L or R. When you see a farm building off to the L, where a stream crosses under the road, the road veers round to the R and shortly afterwards, after three or four more hairpins, the road flattens out and you reach the…

5km Vierge de Biakorri 1095m

A small statue of the Virgin Mary in a prominent position at the side of a road junction and in a level area, brought there from Lourdes by shepherds. Panoramic views and a good place for a rest (not too long). At the Vierge de Biakorri you are halfway in time (but not in distance) between Saint-Jean-Pied-de-Port and Roncesvalles. It is still 5km to the border and the route still climbs, though less steeply now, up to the Col de Bentarte, after which it is either fairly level or nearly all downhill. The temperature may be cooler as you climb higher, but the sun will still be as strong.

Be careful to take the R fork here *(the LH option, with wide parking area, leads you back down again!)* and continue on road (having taken R fork) and KSO at road junction (with the D128, R, to Arnéguy). At 1177m pass the 'remains' of **Château Pignon** (L). Ignore a turn to L after 300m and also a fork to R after 300m (to a farm 100m off road).

Continue on road until it begins to veer round to L, at which point the *camino* leaves the road to the R (at 1240m) up a clearly marked grassy track by a cairn and then the **Croix Thibaut,** *a modern wayside cross erected in 1990 on the RH side of the road with an inscription in Basque ('I am the way...').* However, although the point at which you leave the road is indicated clearly enough, at the time the present edition of this guide was being prepared, this section was not well *waymarked at all until the Spanish border. There are some red and white balises on the ground but you will mainly have to follow the track that is clearly marked by heavy use, particularly in poor visibility.*

The D428 continues for another 3km to the border at the Col d'Arnostéguy, more or less on the level, before it comes to a dead end. However, if you get caught unexpectedly in foggy weather you can continue along this road and then backtrack along the border fence until you reach marker no 199 and where the terrain is slightly shaded.

When you see the border fence, to your R, go down towards it, after which the track become very clear, and reach the Spanish border at the...

5km Col de Bentarte 1337m

Once over the border pass a fountain (L) and the yellow arrows start – very large and extremely clearly *(some people may consider them 'overkill' but they are needed for safety).* KSO on a wide, clearly-marked track for 4km until, 150m after a cattle grid, you reach a minor road, the...

4km Col Lepoeder 1440m

From here you have the first, plunging view of the rooftops of the abbey at Roncesvalles down in the valley below, the village of Burguete and, on a clear day, right across into the province of Navarra. You may find remains of snow here, even in early June.

Cross the road, go down a stony FP and 60m later reach a junction. Here you have a choice as there are, in fact, two routes down to Roncesvalles, both of them well waymarked and both described here.

a) Turn L for the 'short, sharp' option. This goes via a **Calzada Romana** (an old Roman road) and is very steep, describing a 'J'-shaped loop straight down to the abbey in Roncesvalles. It passes to the L of the hill known as Don Simon and drops over 500m (1600ft) in only 3.5km (2 miles). When you reach the bottom turn R to enter the abbey from the west (the back). Cross diagonally through a courtyard and pass in front of the church in **Roncesvalles**.

b) Turn R for the slightly longer (4.2km), less steep option. This takes you via the **Puerta de Ibañeta**. Go down a grassy track and then a stony FP to a small road coming from back L. KSO(R) along it. After 1km look out for (waymarked) short cuts to its hairpins. After several of these fork L downhill to side of road, continue through woods and rejoin road 500m later at U-bend and KSO(L) downhill.

Around 300m later fork L off road again and when you return to it the way-mark indicates that you should cross over for a steep 'short cut'. However, it is just as easy to turn L on the road (NA 2033) here, veering R, and pick up the waymarks again 300–400m later. After this you will see the chapel at **Ibañeta** below you and the path down to it clearly indicated.

Continue as described at the top of page 186*.

Roncesvalles (Orreaga) 925m

Shop with guidebooks and so on, hotel-restaurant, monastery-run *posada* (hotel, with ATM inside), youth hostel (35 pl). Walker pilgrims (they have preference over cyclists) may stay in the refuge in the old hospital building (120+pl, open all year, run by volunteer wardens Easter–Nov) after having their '*credencial*' (pilgrim passport) stamped in the pilgrim office in the monastery. Mass every evening in the church, followed by pilgrim blessing.

Augustinian monastery and hospital founded early in the 12th century. Set in the 'valley of thorns' in the foothills of the Pyrenees, it has a long tradition of looking after pilgrims (feeding 25,000 a year during the 17th century). Collegiate church chapel of Santiago, 14th-century royal pantheon containing the 13th-century tombs of Sancho the Strong and his wife Doña Clemencia of Toulouse. Museum with religious paintings and sculpture, treasury.

The whole section from Roncesvalles to shortly before the outskirts of Pamplona is shady in the main and so can be walked comfortably even in July/August unless you are unusually affected by the heat. There are *refugios* as well as other accommodation en route in Zubiri (22km), Larrasoaña (6km) and Trinidad de Arre (12km, 4km from the centre of Pamplona).

The description of the Spanish section of the pilgrim road to Santiago is given in the sequel to this guide: *Way of St James (Camino de Santiago): Pyrenees–Santiago–Finisterre, a Walker's Guide,* also published by Cicerone Press.

APPENDIX B
Saint-Palais to Irún

This three to four day route enables you to connect up with the start of the *Camino del Norte* in Irún, the route along the north coast of Spain. If you take this you then have the option of 'turning left' later onto *the Camino Primitivo,* joining the *Camino Francés* in Palas do Rei, or continuing further on to turn south after Ribadeo and join the *Camino Francés* two days before Santiago in Arzúa. There are plans to waymark the route from Saint-Palais to Irún.

You will need IGN maps 14450 (Saint-Palais), 1345OT (Cambo-les-Bains) and 1245OT (Hendaye), all at a scale of 1: 25 000.

Saint-Palais (see page 74)

9.5km Harribeltzaguéko

5.5km Armendarits

8km Hélette Hotel-Restaurante Aguerria (05.59.37.62.90)

4km Ospitalia

3km Zahiola

10km Itxassou Hotel-Restaurante du Fronton (05.59.29.75.10)

4.5km Haranéa

2.5km Espelette OT, shops, restaurants, Hotel-Restaurante Euzkadi (05.59.93.91.88)

3.5km Col de Pinodieta 176m

7km Pont d'Amotz

7km Sare Shops

3km Col de Saint-Ignace

3.5km Ascain

5km Bridge over the A63

2.5km Saint-Jean-de-Luz All facilities

10km Hendaye All facilities

1km Irún All facilities

APPENDIX C

GR651 – Variant along the Vallée du Célé

This is not the historic route but a pleasant 54km variant along the river Célé until this runs into the Lot in Bouziès and where it joins the GR36. From here you can continue (west) for 21km along the common course of the GR36 and GR46 to rejoin the main GR65 in Les Bories-Basses. The routes are waymarked throughout with the usual red-and-white balises.

Note: there are no cash dispensers along this route.

Béduer
Bakery/shop (7/7 in season, X Mon otherwise). Camping Pech Ibert (05.65.40.05.85, gîte d'étape in marquee in summer, caravans, 15/3–15/11, K).

4km Boussac

2km Corn
CH (05.65.40.00.98 & 06.81.94.27.15).

4km Sainte-Eulalie
CH (05.65.50.26.57).

3km Espagnac
Gîte d'étape communal (05.65.11.45.52 & 05.65.40.09.17, 21pl, Easter–31/10, K).

4km Brengues
Bakery/shop, camping municipal (1/7–30/9), Hôtel-Restaurant de la Vallée (05.65.40.02.50, all year X Sat out of season).

4km Saint-Sulpice
Bar-restaurant Le Saint-Sulpice, 7/7 (and gîte to open 2009). Camping municipal 15/4–30/9 (caravan available 15/6–30/9).
CH at Cazals, Route de Pailhès, 3.5km after Saint-Sulpice (05.65.50.07.89).

7km Marcilhac-sur-Célé
2 shops, hotel, 2 restaurants, bar, TO (in season only). Gîte Accueil Saint-Pierre (05.65.50.05.89, 12pl, K). CH Route de Pailhès (05.65.50.07.89). Camping du Pré de Monsieur (April–Oct).

9km Sauliac-sur-Célé

3.5km Château de Cuzals

2.5km Espinières

4km Cabrerets
TO (June–Aug), shop, bakery, 2 hotel-restaurants. Gîte du Barry (05.65.21.32.60, 21pl, April–Oct after 14:30, K). Camping familiale Cantal (May–October).

5.5km Conduché

1.5km Bouziès
Gîte (05.65.31.28.43 & 06.20.90.74.27, 10pl, 15/3–1/12, K).

4km Saint-Cirq-Lapopie
TO, 7 restaurants, shop, gîte d'étape communal La Fourdonne (05.65.31.21.51, 23pl, Easter–15/11, K). 2 CH a) 05.65.31.49.10 & 06.12.29.76.55, b) 06.35.37.43.39. 2 hotels. Camping de la Plage (all year, bar Easter–Oct).

From here you continue on the GR36–46 to rejoin the GR65 in Les Bories-Basses.

10km Concots
Shop, hotel/restaurant.

7km Les Bories-Basses

APPENDIX D

St James's and other Pilgrim References

Le Puy-en-Velay

- Statue of St James by pillar to RH side of cathedral (facing altar)
- Tiny modern statue of pilgrim in niche above Hôtellerie du Fauçon, Rue des Farges
- Statue of St James in niche above chemist's shop on corner of Rue Saint-Jacques and Place du Plô
- Musée Crozatier contains:
  - two paintings with St James pilgrim in background,
  - a woodcut of St James pilgrim,
  - a statue of Saint-Roch,
  - a small collection of *coquilles* and statues originally housed in the former pilgrim hospital.
- Ceramic roundel (modern) of St James and headless pilgrim on stone calvary along Rue Saint-Jacques leaving Le Puy
- Large wooden statue of St James as pilgrim on L at the top of the Rue des Capucins on leaving Le Puy

Montbonnet

- Chapelle Saint-Roch, early 13th-century Romanesque chapel, the first of many along the way dedicated to the patron saint of pilgrims. It was originally dedicated to St James, then Saint-Bonnet (a local saint) and then, in the 17th century, to Saint-Roch. (Many chapels originally dedicated to St James changed their dedication due to Saint-Roch's success in curing plague victims.)
- Chapel contains two engravings and one statue of Saint-Roch pilgrim.

Saint-Christophe-sur-Dolaison

- Church contains free-standing statue of Saint-Roch with pilgrim staff and scallop shells on shoulders.

Rochegude

- Tiny chapel dedicated to St James, perched on top of rocky belvedere with wooden statue of St James inside

Monistrol-d'Allier

- Headless bas-relief of pilgrim on cross in churchyard of Saint-Marcellin

Saugues

- Town was meeting point of pilgrims coming from the Auvergne via secondary routes and had 12th-century pilgrim hospital (now an old people's home near the Chapelle des Pénitents) dedicated to St James. Large wooden polychrome statue of St James inside (visits possible).
- Stained-glass Saint-Roch in church of Saint-Médard and niche statue high up above west portal
- Niche statue of Saint-Roch in nearby street
- 'Tree' sculpture of pilgrims leaving Saugues by river

Fontaine Saint-Roch (after Domaine du Sauvage, 200m before chapel)

- Site of a 13th-century oratory and pilgrim hospital

Chapelle Saint-Roch (3km after Domaine du Sauvage)

- Also known as Chapelle de l'Hospitalet du Sauvage, this was a hospital for pilgrims and travellers founded at this col in 1198, originally dedicated to St James (chapel was next to present fountain). The chapel was rededicated to Saint-Roch after the Wars of Religion (1562–98) but then fell into ruin. The new chapel, built at the end of the 19th century, was destroyed by a cyclone in 1897 and the present one rebuilt in 1901.
- Statue of Saint-Roch as a pilgrim, with stick, calebasse and scallop shells on hat and clothing, above the altar (visible through the grille in the door)

Les Estrets

- Church contains statue of Saint-Roch inside; lectern has carvings of scallop shell, scrip and pilgrim staff.
- Village formerly had a pilgrim hospital.

Aumont-Aubrac

- Niche of south wall of church of Saint-Etienne has shaft of cross with tiny pilgrim carved on it.

La Chaze-du-Peyre

- Church with (former?) St James's chapel; statue of pilgrim-looking figure with *coquille*, blessing another figure

Nasbinals

- 11th-century Romanesque church with statue of Saint-Roch and (modern wood) Saint-Jacques inside

aint-Chély d'Aubrac
15th-century church
- a stained glass window of Saint-Roch as pilgrim to L of apse
- a gold statue of Saint-Roch pilgrim to LH side of wall behind altar, with a lot of scallop shells on his lapel
- a statue of Saint-Jacques (among other apostles)

Old bridge over the river Boralde has 16th-century cross, with pilgrim sculpted in its base, with his stick and rosary.

aint-Côme d'Olt
Pilgrim hospital dedicated to St James adjoining Chapelle des Pénitents
Ouradou (pilgrim oratory)

spalion
Pilgrim bridge over the Lot
Stained glass St Aléxius dressed as a pilgrim with staff and *coquilles* in parish church

staing
15th-century church of Sainte-Fleuret has stone cross outside depicting tiny pilgrim and gilded statue of St James inside.

olinhac
Church of Saint-Martin has statue of Saint-Roch (with *coquilles*) inside
Cross at entry to village has tiny pilgrim and staff on its base
ote: France has 3674 churches dedicated to St Martin!

speyrac
Church of Saint-Pierre has statue of Saint-Roch pilgrim inside.

énergues
Church of Saint-Martin has statue of Saint-Roch pilgrim inside.

ontromieu
A farm whose name indicates the site of a former 'pilgrim fountain'

Saint-Marcel
- Stained-glass windows above door of church of Saint-Marcel has three scallop shells.
- Leprosarium here in 17th and 18th centuries and a Chapelle Saint-Roch built in 1629 at the height of the plague
- In 1997 a statue of Saint-Roch was to be found inside the church (with hat, scallops, stick and gourd – as a pilgrim), but in 2009 it was no longer there – any information welcome.

Conques
- Chapelle Saint-Roch, perched on top of hill in lower town
- Modern wood Saint-Jacques in abbey church
- Painting and statue of Saint-Roch in front of abbey church in museum

Chapelle Sainte-Foy (part way uphill leaving Conques)
- Modern stained-glass window inside depicting St James the pilgrim

Chapelle Saint-Roch (near Noailhac)
- Statue of Saint-Roch as pilgrim outside on tympanum
- Another statue of the saint (not as a pilgrim) is inside, above the altar

Chapelle Saint-Roch (2km after Decazeville)
- A parish church, rather than the usual chapel/hermitage dedicated to Saint-Roch
- Two statues of the saint inside, one above the main altar in full pilgrim gear
- Two other statues of the saint in the side chapel, one as a pilgrim (minus hat), the other a small alabaster figure as non-pilgrim, to side of altar
- There is also a modern drawing of Saint-Roch the pilgrim on the move, walking with his dog but his cloak is down, covering his sore.

Saint-Félix
- Romanesque church of Sainte-Radegonde has later stained-glass window of St James.

Saint-Jean Mirabel
- Framed painting of a very sturdy-looking Saint-Roch inside church on R
- Modern stained-glass pilgrim window above altar in church with rucksack, stick and gourd

ajarc

Pilgrim bridge over the Lot built in 1320
Pilgrim hospital existed in 1269.

ahors

15th-century cloister in cathedral of Saint-Etienne has sculpture of small pilgrim apparently disagreeing violently with another non-identified figure.
Cahors formerly had four hospitals (one dedicated to St James) and a Chapelle de Saint-Jacques des Pénitents.

ascabanes

Pilgrim hospital in the 15th century

Moissac

Ruins of Hôpital Saint-Jacques
Former church of St James is now used as Musée Saint Jacques.
Bas-relief of Saint-Jacques (apostle) on corner pillar of abbey cloister

uvillar

Rue Saint-Jacques

auzerte

Modern statue of St James pilgrim inside church of Saint-Barthélmy

Miradoux

Church has modern statue of St James pilgrim.

ectoure

Cathedral of SS Gervais and Protais has stained-glass window of St James.
Town formerly had a Hôpital Saint-Jacques.

Marsolan

Remains of Hôpital Saint-Jacques at entrance to village

hapelle d'Abrin

Former pilgrim hospital (now a private house) at meeting of two routes (the other came from Rocamadour and Moissac via Agen)

La Romieu
- Village taking its name from the *romieux* (pilgrims) who passed through on their way to Santiago
- Gilded bust of Saint-Jacques in Collégiale

Condom
- Eglise Saint-Jacques on leaving town (statue over blocked up doorway is St Joseph, not St James), originally with a hospital behind it. There was also a second Hôpital Saint-Jacques nearby.

Pont d'Artigues
- Pilgrim hospital by the bridge over the Osse, run by the Order of the Knights of Santiago in the Middle Ages

Eauze
- Statue of Saint-Roch pilgrim in a side chapel in church of Saint-Luperc
- Stained-glass Saint-Jacques in apse and stained-glass Saint-Roch on south wall

Manciet
- La Bonne Auberge (restaurant) is on the site of the former commandery (with Hôpital Saint-Jacques and chapel) set up by the Order of the Knights of Santiago.
- Modern statue of Saint-Jacques above church portal and statue of Saint-Roch inside

Nogaro
- Romanesque church with former Hôpital Saint-Jacques nearby
- Medieval paintings of pilgrims inside church of Saint-Nicolas

Lanne-Soubiran
- Wooden polychrome statue of St James the pilgrim in church of Saint-Pierre

Eglise de Sensacq
- 11th-century church formerly dedicated to St James

Arzacq-Arraziguet
- Stained-glass window of St James in parish church of Saint-Pierre

Louvigny
- Modern church of Saint-Martin has stained-glass window with *coquille* and pilgrim staff and gourd.

omps
Eglise Saint-Jacques (with statue of the saint)

Castillon
Hospital for pilgrims and travellers in 11th century

Chapelle de Caubin
Garden of restored Romanesque chapel contains sculpture recalling the passage of pilgrims en route to Santiago.

a Sauvelade
• Church of St James (originally dedicated to St Mary) is all that is left of monastery, with statue of St James inside.

Navarrenx
• Church of Saint-Germain has pilgrim boss at base of ceiling vaulting near side chapel to RH side, with head with leather hat and scallop shell; three other heads believed to be of modern pilgrims.

Aroue
• Romanesque church of Saint-Etienne has 12th-century bas-reliefs of Santiago Matamoros in lintel on sacristy doors.

aint-Palais
• Musée de la Basse Navarre et des Chemins de Saint-Jacques de Compostelle contains statue of St James the pilgrim and much other historic pilgrim material from the region, including a copy of the bas-relief of Santiago Matamoros from Aroue church (which is often closed).

arribar-Sorhapuru
• Shrine to R of four-arched bridge over the Bidouze with small statue of St James behind glass in a *stèle*

Hiriburia
• Monument erected by the Société des Amis de Saint-Jacques to mark the place where the routes from Paris, Vézelay and Le Puy are thought to have met

Harambeltz
• Statue of St James inside chapel

Ostabat-Asme

- Important pilgrim gathering point in past for those coming from or along different routes and its inns and hospitals could accommodate up to 5000 pilgrims; today only the Maison Ospitalia remains, as the present gîte d'étape.

Saint-Jean-Pied-de-Port

- Porte Saint-Jacques, through which pilgrims entered the town
- Formerly there was also a Chapelle St Jacques.

APPENDIX E

Suggestions for Further Reading

General

Attwood, Donald and John, C.R.
Penguin Dictionary of Saints, 3rd edn
(Harmondsworth: Penguin, 1995)

Coleman, Simon and Elsner, John.
Pilgrimage past and present in the World's Religions
(London: British Museum Press, 1995)

Davies, J.G.
Pilgrimage yesterday and today: why? where? how?
(London: SCM Press, 1988)

Studies the nature of pilgrimages and motives behind them, from patristic times to the Middle Ages, Protestant condemnation of pilgrimages and the 19th-century revival of pilgrimages amongst Protestants, ending with a review of the devotional aspects of modern pilgrmages.

Frey, Nancy Louise.
Pilgrim Stories
(Berkley & Los Angeles: University of California Press, 1998)

This refers specifically to the experiences of modern pilgrims along the road to Santiago de Compostela, before, during and after after making their pilgrimage, but the questions raised confront any modern pilgrim on a route where the journey itself, rather than the destination, is the real issue at stake.

Robinson, Martin.
Sacred Places, Pilgrim Paths: an anthology of pilgrimage
(London: Fount, 1997)

An anthology reflecting the experiences of pilgrims through the ages, dealing with places of pilgrimage, preparation for the journey, the journey itself, the inner journey, worship on the way and on arrival and the questions raised once the pilgrimage is over.

Sumption, Jonathan.
Pilgrimage
(London: Faber and Faber, 1975)

A study of the traditions of pilgrimage prevalent in Europe from the beginning of Christianity to the end of the 15th century, examining all its aspects: major destinations, motivations, the cult of the saints and their relics, medicine and the quest for cures, penitential pilgrimage, the practicalities of the journey and the pilgrims themselves.

Eade, John and Sallnow, Michael J. (eds)
Contesting the Sacred: the anthropology of Christian pilgrimage
(London: Routledge, 1991)

Contributors examine particular Christian shrines (in France, Italy, Israel, Sri Lanka and Peru), analysing the dynamics of religious expression and belief but also the political and economic processes at local and global levels, emphasising that pilgrimage is primarily an arena for competing religious and secular discourses.

French, R.M. (trans)
The Way of a Pilgrim
(London: Triangle, 1995)

First published in English in 1930 this book was written by an unknown Russian pilgrim in the 19th century, telling the story of his wanderings from one holy place to another in Russia and Siberia in search of the way of prayer.

Way of St James

Barret, Pierre and Gurgand, Jean-Noël.
Priez pour nous à Compostelle
(Paris: Hachette, 1978)

An account of the authors' journey from Vézelay to Santiago on foot, interspersed with parallel accounts of pilgrims from previous centuries. Contains a very extensive bibliography.

Bourdarias, Jean and Wasielewski, Michel.
Guide Européen des Chemins de Compostelle
(Paris: Fayard, 1997)

Guide to all the European routes to Santiago (from Holland, Denmark, Poland, Hungary, Brenner, Croatia, Italy and Portugal), as well as the currently more well-known routes through France and Spain. Contains maps, distances, over 800 photographs, history and descriptions of places, lives of saints and relevant Biblical extracts.

Mullins, Edward.
The Pilgrimage to Santiago
(London: Secker & Warburg, 1974, and London: Sigma Books, 2001)

An account of the art, architecture, history and geography of the pilgrim route from Paris to Santiago.

Neillands, Rob.
The Road to Compostela
(Ashbourne: Moorland Publishing Co, 1985)

An account of the author's journey from Le Puy to Santiago by bicycle.

Shaver-Crandell, Annie and Gerson, Paula.
The Pilgrim's Guide to Santiago de Compostela: a Gazeteer
(London/Langhorne: Harvey Miller, 1995)

Contains 730 entries and 575 illustrations describing all the relics of saints, important monuments, towns and buildings encountered by the 12th-century pilgrim along the four main routes through France and then in Spain. Includes a new translation of the Latin text of the *Codex Calixtinus* plus discussion of the pilgrimage phenomenon in the Middle Ages as well as the tradition of travel literature.

Tate, Brian and Marcus.
The Pilgrim Route to Santiago
(Oxford: Phaidon, 1987)

Explains the pilgrim phenomenon and the history of the shrine as well as discussing the different routes. Contains 137 photographic illustrations by Pablo Keller, 60 of them in colour.

Viellard, Jeanne.
Guide du Pèlerin de Saint Jacques de Compostelle
(Paris: Klincksieck, 4th edn 1989)

A French translation, on facing pages, of what is probably the first known guide book: Aymery Picaud's 12th-century description of the pilgrim routes to Santiago

The Pilgrim's Guide: a 12th-century Guide for the Pilgrim to St James of Compostela, translated from the Latin by James Hogarth
(Confraternity of St James, 1992)

En Chemin vers Saint Jacques: guide spirituel du pèlerin
(Conques [Communauté des Prémontrés]/Estaing [Hospitalité Saint Jacques] 2001)

Pocket-size (A6) booklet intended as a spiritual aid, containing themes for personal meditation, prayers and hymns and notes on the many saints whose churches, chapels and sanctuaries line the route.

APPENDIX F
Useful Addresses

Confraternity of Saint James
27 Blackfriars Road
London SE1 8NY

Tel: (020) 7928 9988
email: office@csj.org.uk
www.csj.org.uk
online bookshop:
www.csj.org.uk/bookshop

The Confraternity also has a picture gallery on its website, including an extensive collection from the Le Puy route.

Stanfords
12 Long Acre
Covent Garden
London WC2E 9LP

Tel: (020) 7836 1321
www.stanfords.co.uk

The Map Shop
15 High Street
Upton-upon-Severn
Worcestershire
WR8 0HJ

Tel: (01684) 593146
www.themapshop.co.uk

Editions du Vieux Crayon
(for the *Miam Miam Dodo* guide)
119 Route de l'Aubraie
85100 Les Sables d'Olonne
France

Tel: (00 33) 2.51.90.84.97
info@levieuxcrayon.com
j.clouteau@wanadoo.fr

Factage E2R
www.factage.free.fr

Transbagages
www.transbagages.com

APPENDIX G
Glossary

balise	waymark
barry	suburb (Occitan)
bastide	walled hilltop town
borie	farm (Occitan)
buron	shepherd's bothy
calade	paved road or path (Occitan)
carriera	street (Occitan)
caselle	small round hut of drystone construction
chasse gardée	private ground/hunting
causse	limestone plateau in south-west France with scrubby vegetation
château d'eau	water tower
cledo	flexible gate made of wire and palings
col	mountain pass
commanderie	commandery (of military order)
couderc	enclosed field/village green (Gascon)
draille	drove road
écluse	(canal) lock
fronton	pelota court (Basque country)
gave	mountain stream/river in the Pyrenees
gaviote	stone hut, similar to *caselle*
halle	(covered) market place
hameau	hamlet
jacquet	pilgrim going to Santiago
lavoir	outdoor washing-place, (public) wash-house
lieu-dit	locality
luy	river (Gascon)

Mairie	town hall, town council
mas	house/farm in south of France (Occitan)
mirador	watchtower, mirador
montjoie	cairn
montredon	rounded hill (Occitan)
palombière	hide in forest used by pigeon-hunters
passage canadien	cattle grid
passerelle	footbridge
patte d'oie	junction
pech	hill, mountain (Occitan)
pèlerin	pilgrim
pigeonnier	dovecote
puy	hill, mountain
réserve de chasse	hunting preserve
romieu	pilgrim (especially one who has been to Rome)
sauvetat/sauveté/sauveterre	town or area serving as safe haven
tampon	(rubber) stamp
temple	Protestant church

For those pilgrims who like to attend mass and would like to be able to participate at least once during the service, the text of the Lord's Prayer is given here:

Notre Père qui es aux cieux,
que ton nom soit sanctifié,
que ton règne vienne,
que ta volonté soit faite
sur la terre comme au ciel.
Donne-nous aujourd'hui
notre pain de ce jour.
Pardonne-nous nos offenses,
comme nous pardonnons aussi
à ceux qui nous ont offensés.
Et ne nous soumets pas à la tentation,
mais délivre-nous du Mal.

APPENDIX H

Index of Principal Place Names

APPENDIX I
Index of Maps

APPENDIX J
Summary of Route

NOTES

NOTES

NOTES

NOTES

LISTING OF CICERONE GUIDES

For full information on all
our guides, and to order
books and eBooks, visit our
website:
www.cicerone.co.uk.

Walking – Trekking – Mountaineering – Climbing – Cycling

Over 40 years, Cicerone have built up an outstanding collection of 300 guides, inspiring all sorts of amazing adventures.

Every guide comes from extensive exploration and research by our expert authors, all with a passion for their subjects. They are frequently praised, endorsed and used by clubs, instructors and outdoor organisations.

All our titles can now be bought as **e-books** and many as iPad and Kindle files and we will continue to make all our guides available for these and many other devices.

Our website shows any **new information** we've received since a book was published. Please do let us know if you find anything has changed, so that we can pass on the latest details. On our **website** you'll also find some great ideas and lots of information, including sample chapters, contents lists, reviews, articles and a photo gallery.

It's easy to keep in touch with what's going on at Cicerone, by getting our monthly **free e-newsletter**, which is full of offers, competitions, up-to-date information and topical articles. You can subscribe on our home page and also follow us on **Facebook** and **Twitter**, as well as our **blog**.

Cicerone – the very best guides for exploring the world.

CICERONE

2 Police Square Milnthorpe Cumbria LA7 7PY
Tel: 015395 62069 info@cicerone.co.uk
www.cicerone.co.uk